Diary of a Psychic

Laura Powers

LAURA
POWERS
PUBLISHING

LAURA
POWERS
PUBLISHING

Acknowledgements

I'd like to recognize my spirit guides, angels and those who helped me along the way. I wouldn't be here without the support of my family, especially my mother, who is always an inspiration to me. I also want to thank my grandmother, grandfather and great-grandmother (who I am named after) on the other side. I want to thank my sister, all my aunts, uncles, and of course cousins who were there for me. My friends have been there in times and in ways that I didn't expect and this goes out to all of them – you know who you are! This book is also dedicated to my soul family on the other side including the souls of Marilyn Monroe, Frank Sinatra, Michael Jackson, Dean Martin, and so many others who have helped me with guidance from the other side.

Dedication

This book is dedicated to everyone out there who has psychic gifts, whether or not they know it (this probably means you)! This book is for all of those who are psychic, think they might be psychic, and yes even those who want to be psychic but think they aren't. This world is full of psychic people and this book is for you.

Special Thanks

A special thank you to all those who contributed and pre-ordered copies of this book; without you, this book wouldn't have been possible. Thank you to the following:

Christine O'Neill, Christine Webb, Claire Grasso, Don Cory, Erica Bridgeman, James Anderson, Jan Lund, Kara Massoletti, Laura Baalman, Louisa Meyer, Meyers Family, Norman Plotkin, Paul Nicholas, Rupal Patel, Sharon Cooper, Sherry Bertram, Tom Metcalf, Tricia Carr, and Wade Vernon.

Table of Contents

Introduction

I was inspired to write this book based on a Facebook post I made while traveling to Paris on the way to host "The Dark Side of Paris" tour. During a layover at JFK airport, I noticed how many people had demon and dark entity (energy beings that feed on dark energy) attachments. I was frustrated that they sat very close to me when other seats were available. They attacked me which I had to deal with and it was annoying and distracting. I made a Facebook post about it and a funny conversation ensued about this situation. I realized that I had lots of stories to tell about the odd aspects of being a psychic. Living my life seeing and sensing what I do, I realize that my day to day happenings, struggles, challenges and joys are different than most peoples. In this book, I share stories about my life, some of them funny and some of them sad. I also reveal information I have learned about the after-life, karma, reincarnation, and other aspects of the psychic realm. This is not an instructional book, but I think that through these stories,

1

a lot can be learned as well. I hope that you laugh at my mistakes and enjoy the quirkier aspects of what it is like to be me.

Let me provide a quick note about how to read this book. You can read the first couple of chapters in which I talk about my background, how I got to be a psychic, and the psychic world, in general, or you can just skip right to the stories. However, you go about reading this book, I hope you enjoy it. Happy reading!

ONE
What is a Psychic?

The term psychic is often misunderstood, so I thought I would start this book right away by talking about what a psychic is and what a psychic is not. Often when I meet people who have learned I am a psychic, they thrust out their hand at me and ask me to read their palm. As it turns out, I am not a palm reader, though I did do palm readings for fun as a child. I also get asked to read auras, which I also do not do. Generally speaking, a psychic is a person who gets information from the non-physical realm or through their psychic senses. There are many different forms of psychic ability such as clairvoyance (psychic seeing), clauraudience (psychic hearing), clairsentience (psychic feeling), and a whole host of others. You can have psychometry which means you get information through the sense of touch. Or you can have precognitive (future telling) dreams. There are also psychics who use different forms of divination to receive information. This means that they use various psychic tools such as tarot or oracle cards, tea leaves, etc. to get information. Though I don't do it, there are many psychics that do read auras too. I am sure there are many more types of psychics that I am missing, but the types I have listed give you a sense of the various ways psychic abilities can be used.

I also want to talk about what a psychic is not. A psychic is not all knowing. If we were all-knowing, we would probably not be incarnated any more, we would be closer to God. We do have more information than most people, but we cannot always control what information comes through. Basically, we are getting the information from angels and spirit guides and the world around us. Unless those guides release the information to us somehow, we will not have it. For example, if you ask me for the winning lottery numbers and your guides do not think it is a good idea for you to have those numbers, then they will not be told to me. Also, to make matters even more complex, the future is always in flux. There are certain things that are quite likely, but most things are in a constant state of change. Everything that we think, do, or say has a ripple or butterfly affect changing everything else. Some things have a greater impact than others, but even simple things such as which outfit you wear, which way you go to work, or what restaurant you go to have a much greater impact than you might think. This means that even if I tell you that something is going to happen in two weeks and tomorrow you get a wild hair and book a flight to Timbuktu, that future I foresaw will likely not come to pass. All in all, it is quite a complex situation.

Psychics also do not know everything about ourselves either. We cannot psychically see everything that relates to ourselves because we are still incarnated and learning what we came here to learn. If we knew everything in regards to ourselves, we wouldn't be able to experience life as we need to in order to learn and grow. It is true that I know more about my future and my

4

past than most people, but still there are pieces that are unclear about my own path.

That said, there are insights that psychics can give you which can be quite helpful to you so long as you use the information responsibly but don't get too reliant on it. I am going to let you in on a little secret. Everyone is at least a little psychic. Similarly, almost anyone can create some kind of painting or drawing. There are, however, varying levels of natural ability. No amount of training is going to make everyone a Picasso or a Van Gogh. Many people have astounding natural affinity but have never picked up a psychic paint brush, so-to-speak. My mother is incredibly psychic, but did not realize it until she started taking classes and then recognizing her gifts.

In my opinion, a good psychic can give you extra insight into not only what is coming for you but how you can change the outcome of future events. A psychic can help identify what blocks you might have as well as your karma, past lives, and who your spirit guides are. A psychic is not meant to be used as a crutch, however. I believe a good psychic will help empower you to see things more clearly and navigate a better life.

Another misconception about psychics is the manner in which psychic gifts come through. Each person's gifts are different and even the same gift can manifest differently at different times. Essentially, it is not easy to predict or control the gifts. For me, the gifts come through as they do and all I can do is remain receptive and open. The moment I try to manage it all, it blocks the channel. For example, sometimes I see spirits or entities psychically and occasionally I see them in the physical plane. If I "try" to see them in the physical plane when they are not naturally manifesting that way, I will likely simply get a headache and feel frustrated. In many ways, psychic gifts are like water in that water goes where it will.

Forcing water to go uphill is very difficult. I find it much easier to simply go with the flow and see where the water is taking me.

People often assume that what I do is a trick. I understand this can be very confusing as there are many magician mentalists that pretend to read minds, etc. There are also many fake psychics. Harry Houdini, the famed magician, wanted to believe in psychics, but every time he came across one, he was able to demystify them and prove that they were using tricks. This has frustrated me as there are real psychics and the more charlatans there are out there, the harder it is to believe anyone is real. Part of each person's responsibility is to determine for themselves who is real and who is not.

There are also those who think that psychics are scientifically impossible. Those are usually the ones who will corner me at a party and start arguing with me. I don't have time for that, so I usually excuse myself and say that we will simply have to disagree. I do believe that at some point science will confirm undeniably that psychic abilities do exist, though the evidence may be more subtle than what is in the physical realm. If you'd like to read more about current science that backs up psychic abilities, you can read the book *The Intention Experiment*.

The last misconception I'd like to clear up is about what a psychic looks like. I cannot tell you how often clients will meet me and tell me how surprised they are by how I look. I do not wear a turban or lots of scarves and I am not a gypsy. A psychic can look just like anyone else. I model in addition to working as a psychic and so I really do not look like the stereotype of a psychic. A psychic can look like anyone. You cannot tell a psychic from a non-psychic just by looking at them, unless of course you are psychic yourself and are getting information from the non-physical realm. My hope is that through my work and through media, that people will open their eyes to psychic phenomena in the world and in themselves. After all, I have not always thought I was psychic, I used to think I was crazy. More on that in the next chapter.

TWO
How I Got to be a Psychic

I did not set out to be a psychic, I don't think anybody sets out to be a psychic or at least they probably didn't when they were little. When little kids are dreaming about what they are going to do, no little boys or girls that I've ever known have said, "I want to be a psychic." Perhaps with shows like *Medium* and *Ghost Whisperer* that is changing, but when I was a girl, there was nothing farther from my mind. I didn't even have a model for psychics or a concept of them based in non-stereotypes. Though my family is very psychic, none of them were practicing psychics and none of them even knew about psychic gifts and how they work. It was not until I was an adult that I fully understood my gifts and that I could use these gifts on purpose.

Growing up, I wondered if maybe I was crazy! I regularly saw and sensed spirits that no one else did. The only logical conclusion I could come to at the time was that it was all in my head which was not a very comforting conclusion. In fact, a lot of those who later became psychics have had past lives where we've been persecuted for our gifts (more on that later). That is partially because those who have psychic gifts often have soul gifts. Did you know that certain traits are not just a part of who you are in this life but part of who you are as a soul? For example, those who are musical have usually been musical in past lives. Often, those who are young geniuses learn so quickly because they have mastered their art previously in one or more lives.

At any rate, I was afraid to talk about my gifts because of past life persecutions and also because it appeared that others around me did not sense the non-physical things that I did. I could tell because no one reacted to them, I often looked at them to be sure. Once I even checked with my mother to see if she knew what I was talking about. I asked if she saw things and I could tell by her answer that she did not. So for many years, decades even, I kept it all to myself and did my best to ignore all of this stuff from the spiritual world.

I later confirmed that I wasn't crazy because a family friend described a ghost that he encountered at our house, a ghost that I had seen but told nobody about. Still, I was unsure how to handle this newfound knowledge that indeed the things I sensed were real. If you want to read more about my journey, you can read more about it in my book, *Life and the After-Life: Notes from a Medium and Angel Communicator*. I did my best to cope for a couple of years and then did the only thing I knew how to do, I shut it all out. This seemed to work great until I married a man who was anything but honest. I became sick emotionally and physically, and on top of that I was even unemployed. Basically, my life was a mess. I went to a psychic myself since I was at a loss for how to move forward. The experience changed my life and got me to open up, reach out to the angels for help, and altered my life dramatically. I am so glad this happened. In retrospect, I am thankful for all the experiences I had that helped me get to the point where I am today. At the time though, I felt I was in crisis.

It was through this experience that I began to understand the importance of receiving helpful information through our psychic senses. I took psychic development classes and read voraciously. I was determined not to let the same thing happen to me again. I got a divorce, moved to Shanghai for a year, and everything in my life changed. I embraced the psychic lifestyle for myself but resisted becoming a professional psychic. There was a part of me that believed it was too good to be true and there was another part of me that feared ridicule, judgment, and even persecution. Slowly with my angels and spirit guides, I worked through these fears and began working as a professional psychic. They helped me so much along the way. One thing about working as a psychic is that you see the world with new eyes and with a broader perspective. The information I have learned as a psychic, about myself and the world, is invaluable. I wouldn't trade it for anything. So, it often is that the things we resist the most are the things that are the best for us in the end. The rest of this book includes some of what I have learned. Many of these things are entertaining, some are surprising. I hope they give you a little window into what it's like when you see and sense ghosts, angels, spirits, faeries, and other supernatural creatures. Life is never boring in my world.

THREE
The Psychic World

I often tell people that I live in the magic world while some live in the muggle world (the non-magical world described in *Harry Potter*). For those in the muggle world, ghosts, angels, witches, vampires, and dragons are a thing of fiction. For me, all of these beings are real. For many, there is comfort in thinking of these beings as fiction. I understand that. The idea that these beings are real can be scary though they also bring magic, mystery and wonder. Though there is the potential for darkness, there is also incredible light. In my case, I was thrust into these worlds and there was no denying their existence for me, the only thing I could do was cope. Thankfully, there is so much more to this world than the tough aspects. As I have grown, I have learned how to be safe, how to recognize the signs, and have even benefited from my experiences with the supernatural. I'd like to share with you some of what I've learned about what the world is really like here.

The Invisible World

Less than 400 years ago, if you had told people that they could get sick because of tiny little microbial beings that were as big as a cell, you would have probably been described as crazy. Bacteria were discovered in 1632 and viruses weren't discovered until 1892. Today we accept their existence as fact. What if I were to tell you that just as there are small beings that are invisible to the naked eye and can greatly impact us, so too there are many other larger beings that can impact us and are invisible, not because they are so small, but because they are on a different plane of existence? There are more kinds of beings than I could list, but for the purposes of this book, I will list some of the major types that are there and often interact with us.

Angels

An angel is a being of light whose soul mission and purpose is to help those incarnated. They are light, love, beauty, and caring. They are not pushovers though and are very powerful as well. They can help in ways that most of us can't imagine. They honor our free will and are constantly guiding us, but it's not until we ask that they step in and intervene on our behalf. Their name means 'the watchers' because they are always watching over us. They love us beyond reason. You can read more about angels in my book *Angels: How to Understand, Recognize, and Receive Their Guidance*. Angels are not exclusive to religion though they have been described in all the major world religions. They bring nothing but joy and light into your life. I highly encourage everyone reading to invite their angels into their life right now. You can do this simply by mentally asking your angels in to assist and support you. The spirit world is telepathic so they will hear you. Do this every day and watch your life transform! You cannot bother the angels or talk to them too much. They are not limited by time and space the way that we are since they are not incarnated.

Spirits and Spirit Guides

When I refer to a spirit, I refer to a spirit in the light or who is on the other side. Spirits go to the other side in between incarnations and so they inherently understand more about it than we do. We also have a circle of spirit guide helpers that are constantly guiding, supporting, and communicating with us. Not all spirits are spirit guides, however. We usually have a small group that supports us and the rest are simply doing what they do on the other side. We can ask loved ones in spirit form to come and visit and say hello. They too can hear us in the realm of spirit through our thoughts.

Ghosts

A ghost is an incarnated being whose body has died and whose soul has remained trapped on the physical plane. Since they do not have their body, it is more difficult for them to interact with the physical although some have learned to do so. They are very different from a spirit on the other side because they have not crossed into the light and are therefore lacking information about their life purpose, why the things happened that did, etc. Ghosts are usually not happy people; after all, something kept them from crossing into the light and that something is usually not good. There are occasionally ghosts that are quite content to hang about in the place where they lived, but even then, they are not letting go and moving forward which is what would be the best for them. Ghosts usually don't have the same sense of the passage of time as live people. They might even be stuck in a loop, reliving their end of life or a particular event, over and over again. Ghosts, generally speaking, don't have the full picture, so I never recommend asking a ghost for advice as they are simply unqualified. It would be like asking advice from someone who's in a really bad place in their life....it is not a good idea!

Dark Entities and Demons

The world is full of opposites. Dark entities and demons are the polar opposite of angels. They feed on and create despair, struggle, anger, depression, malaise, pain, heaviness, etc. There is a big difference between angels and these beings. Just like a nice person will wait until being invited to go into your house, a not-nice person will not care how you feel. They will break into your house, steal your stuff, and not care how you feel about it. That is how the dark operates. This means that dark entities, demons, and other dark beings don't need to be invited in. They are constantly doing what they want without considering you in the equation. Dark energies and beings will barge into your life until you set your boundaries and remove them. This means that no matter how much you don't want them there, until you take action, they will remain. Imagine you are given a patch of wild land. It will likely be full of weeds. It is not until you go in, remove the weeds, and plant flowers that it will change. Wishing it one way or the other does no good. Our mind, lives, and energy fields are much the same. It is not until we weed, plant and tend to our inner garden that things will change. These dark beings are just around until we enforce boundaries and get them out. This is also why it's important to invite the light in. The dark will simply show up, but the light waits for permission and honors what we choose. Of course, most people don't understand this and then the weeds take over the garden and the flowers are either never planted or are suffocated. If you are in a bad place in your life, it is likely that there are a lot of dark beings around you feeding like parasites on your negative energy. If you'd like to learn more about how they work, you can read my book *Diary of a Ghost Whisperer*.

The basic principle is that anything dark feeds dark entities and brings them in. So activities, behaviors, patterns or belief systems which create pain and struggle, unhappiness, etc. will also draw them in. If you change your patterns, environment, thoughts etc., you will not give them the food they desire and they will move along and leave you alone. The light, however, will always be there. Even in your darkest hour, light beings will stand by your side. You just may not be able to sense these beings if you are surrounded by darkness. Imagine someone giving you words of support and love while an angry person yells in your face. That is what it is like in the spirit realm. We need to remove the dark beings in order to connect with the light and be receptive.

Faeries

Faeries are often misunderstood beings that reside in a different plane than ours but can come into ours as well. Some believe that they used to be in our plane, but then they left to another because of problems with humans. I think there may be something to this. Faeries are elemental beings associated with one of the elements: fire, air, water, and earth. The faerie plane includes what we traditionally think of as faeries as well as other magical creatures such as elves, dragons, mermaids and mermen, etc. Those in the faerie plane are much more connected to the earth and nature as a general rule than humans. Keep in mind that there are light faeries and dark faeries, though most people are likely to come into contact with the light ones in my experience. Generally speaking, they are pretty playful and sometimes mischievous and will only interact with those they trust and feel aligned with. If you see a faerie, it is likely you are connected with them and their realm somehow. Think of it as an honor. There are so many different types of faeries. The ones I have seen the most look reminiscent of Tinkerbell. They look like a little ball of light with a figure inside. Even if you have not seen faeries, you can ask to see them and then be aware. You are likely to see them in nature or in that in-between sleep and dream state when we are the most psychic.

Vampires

Vampires are real even though they are written about as fiction; some things said about them are correct and some are not. Vampires are related to humans but do need blood or energy. They can also eat food though if they do not get blood, although they will not survive for long on food alone. There are humans that think of themselves as vampires and might even crave blood, but there are also supernatural vampires that can do things that humans most decidedly cannot. Vampires can be physically in our plane or they can make themselves invisible and essentially disappear. Other impressive abilities include flying, "glamouring" people (hypnotizing them) and they can also control small animals. As a part of their gift of mind control, they can also erase people's memories. This means that if you've had an encounter with them, you may or may not remember it. Vampires often get a bad rap amongst humans, but I find it helpful to remember that vampires are much like humans;

there are nice humans and not-nice humans. Vampires are the same. When they feed and if they do it with permission, the experience can be ecstatic for both parties. If they feed without permission, it can be violent and unpleasant. Compare the experience of making love or having sex versus rape, there is quite a difference in the experience.

Another thing to think about is that when humans feed on an animal, it dies. However, when a vampire feeds, they may only take a small amount of blood and it may not be detrimental to the individual being fed upon. Contrary to popular belief, they do not need permission to come inside your home. Vampires can be born or they can be made or turned and those that are turned tend to stay on the human plane, but those who are born vampire usually never make it to the human plane at all. There are a small number of vampires that interact with humans on the human plane. As with anyone, it is important to remember that since vampires are people, it is best to use your intuition about whom to connect with or not to connect with. Seeing a real vampire is actually pretty rare for those in the human world. There are some stereotypes that are true. They are often handsome (or beautiful) and dark, they have mesmerizing eyes, and they can be wild and are fairly nocturnal but can be in the sun, although it does drain them energetically. Vampires are very passionate people and whatever they feel, they feel very intensely. They are extremely magical and can manifest and work with the energetic realm quite easily compared with most humans.

Shapeshifters

Shapeshifters, like vampires, are rare for humans to come across. There are different types of shapeshifters but the core aspect that makes them a shapeshifter is the ability to shift from one form to another. A werewolf is a type of shapeshifter though a werewolf can

17

only shift between their human form and their wolf form. There are other types of were creatures as well including wererats and werecats. There are also shapeshifters that can take on just about any form they want to. These beings are very magical and can often be very dangerous. There are some very nice werewolves but as with any being you don't know, proceed with caution. If you get paranoid during the full moon, know that it is not true that were creatures must change during the full moon. They can change when they want to. Emotions and tendencies are intensified during the full moon, so I believe that is where that myth began. Shapeshifters can take over for a person and will look and sound exactly like the individual they have shapeshifted into though, of course, they will still have their own consciousness. There are different types of shapeshifters from different dimensions and planes. I have some experience with shapeshifters, but they are less known to me than ghosts, dark entities, and angels.

The Other Side

You may wonder what happens on the other side. It is a place of beauty, learning and work too. It is the main place souls reside when they are not incarnated. It is also where lives are planned and reviewed. Yes, we do at least attempt to plan our lives when we are born. After we die, we review our lives to see what went well, what we could have done better, etc. It is a place of wonder and just as we can manifest over here, we can manifest over there, though it is much faster. This means that essentially whatever you think about happens almost instantaneously. There is no hunger or pain on the other side. It is a place of beauty and light. On the other side, we connect with our loved ones, enjoy ourselves, as well as plan and review our incarnations.

18

You might wonder why incarnation is necessary. What I have learned is that it is only possible to have soul growth when incarnated. As a soul, you can understand the concept of something, but it is only when you practice it, that you really grasp it. It's a bit like learning about something in school, but then you get into the "real world" and learn it is not as straightforward as it might seem. On the other side, we know and learn principles and then we practice them when we are incarnated. When we incarnate, we forget (generally speaking) who we were before, what we planned, what we are trying to learn, etc. It is this sort of soul amnesia which allows us to make decisions based on what we know and feel and practice deeply. We have all known those who do not practice what they preach. Incarnation allows us to put into practice what we have learned and to learn new soul lessons.

Reincarnation

The term reincarnation refers to the process souls go through to incarnate in physical form after having had previous incarnations. The term inherently means that we have been more than one person. We reincarnate and essentially forget all our soul knowledge on a conscious level and then operate by instinct. Then we die, review our life, plan our next life, and start the process all over again. We might take a break, so that we can have a rest in between incarnations. As far as I understand it, it is simply the way things work until we learn so much as a soul that we don't have to incarnate any more. We do not remember our past lives because it would be overwhelming for us. That said, I have started to remember past lives because I am ready to integrate the information from them. Having all of that information at once could overwhelm us. That is why even when previous lives are revealed, it is done in bits and pieces so that we can process what we need to from each life. Imagine having all of your joys and sorrows from 600 lives heaped upon you at once. It would be overwhelming!

Another fascinating element I learned about reincarnation is that advanced or "older" souls can have more than one incarnation at a time. This means it is possible for us to be more than one person at a time. Indeed, very advanced souls may have a split incarnation of 8 to 10 lives at a time. This is unusual, but it does happen. If you are curious about this, you can read about this in the book *Bringing Your Soul to Light* by Dr. Linda Backman. I also interviewed her on my podcast, *Healing Powers Podcast* which is free and available on iTunes. This is possible because a part of our soul always stays on the other side and manages the process. The possibility of split incarnation also means that you can have overlapping lives. For example, I believe I had concurrent overlapping lives in Paris and in Hollywood. Your incarnated selves are not likely to meet each other, however. Again this is rare to have more than one incarnation at a time, but it does happen.

Soul Development

As we reincarnate and learn lessons, our soul grows, matures, and develops. Just as our physical selves grow and develop, so do our souls. This is challenging because unlike looking at someone's physical body, we cannot identify where a person is at a glance (a baby looks different than an older person). However, with more in depth analysis, it is possible to figure out a person's soul age or development level. There are baby souls. These souls don't really know how to do anything for themselves and need caring and feeding etc. They have much to learn. There are also toddler souls who want to do things for themselves, haven't learned to play nice, and throw temper tantrums when they don't get what they want. Then there are older children who are naïve and maybe moody and temperamental. They may be frustrated that they can't have their way. Teenager souls are very focused on aspects of the material world such as appearance, sex, money, and status. They might also be very disillusioned and struggle with depression and suicide. There are adult souls who have moved past the pure focus on the material world and want deeper meaning in their lives. Parent souls have learned major lessons and are also trying to raise the child souls and help them. Similarly, there are teacher souls who are not directly raising or getting involved with the raising of specific young souls, but are trying to teach larger groups of younger souls. Those who are reaching the mastery level are close to no longer incarnating. They sort of graduate to the other side permanently which means they don't need to keep incarnating because they have learned and practiced all that they need to from the physical plane. This means that they achieved mastery or nearly achieved mastery of life lessons. They are the superstars that we admire for their worldly accomplishments. I would consider Oprah a master teacher. Sir Richard Branson also comes to mind as does Leonardo da Vinci. They are the major influencers that enlighten the world. This is different from those who are simply famous. It is possible to have the head of the class or the popular kids in any soul development group. Many movie and television stars would fall into that category. For example, the Kardashians would be an example of popular kids in the teenage soul age group. Those who are drawn and look up to a particular person are probably just a bit younger or maybe even the same age on a soul level. Of course, age is not exactly the right word but it gets the basic concept of development and maturity across.

Understanding and recognizing these principles is important. You can have a baby soul that is in an eighty-year-old body and a teacher soul in a baby body. There is no point in expecting a baby soul to act like an adult. Would you expect a human baby to? Of course not, they simply haven't grown up yet. However, since we can't see a person's soul age, people often do just that. They get frustrated because people who are very young and undeveloped are not acting maturely. By looking at a person's focus and lifestyle, you can often get a sense of their soul age. This is tricky because we do go through maturation phases in our physical and emotional development as well. That said, we have all seen little kids who are far wiser than their years or old people who are immature and act like little kids.

More advanced and mature souls will start to take a person's soul age into account when determining expectations. This is good for everyone. Can you imagine being a preschooler and being asked to do calculus? It would be unfair and impractical. Also, keep in mind that adult souls are not any better than baby souls. Is a baby bad? No, it just hasn't grown up yet. Judgement has no place here, however, it is important to assess what is likely and actually happening with a particular soul. Hopefully these ideas will give you a different perspective on life and connecting with others.

FOUR
Challenges of Being an Empath

Can you imagine picking up on other people's energies, emotions, and even physical sensations? For years, I assumed that if I felt it, it must be mine, when nothing could have been farther from the truth. What could be worse than feeling everyone else's stuff? Not knowing it wasn't mine. I felt other people's pain, sadness, and even their lust. Since I assumed it was all mine, I thought I was kind of a mess. I remember thinking all the time, "Why am I so sensitive?" Either that or I did what a lot of empaths do and shut down emotionally so I wouldn't be overwhelmed. I was either "too sensitive" or "cold." I felt I couldn't win.

It wasn't until I felt my husband's panic attack from across the country that I was clued in that something strange was going on. I was in Baltimore getting ready for a yoga class and my ex was in Seattle, apparently having a panic attack. I felt nauseated, panicky and had chest constriction. Just a few months' prior, my husband had one of these attacks in front of me and we thought maybe he was having heart problems. It turned out he was under major stress because he was trying to juggle a marriage with me and a new relationship with another woman as if he and I weren't together. He also had a really stressful job. No wonder he was stressed! It was that experience that got me to start putting two and two together. It was a monumental realization for me. I'd lived my whole life, making decisions based on other people's stuff, even medicating for other people's pain. It was such a mind-blowing concept to figure out that what I felt wasn't necessarily mine. Once I figured it out, I really had no idea what to do about it.

I started voraciously reading and searching for information about being an empath and how to handle it. I started working with the angels and asking them for clearing and protection. It was a huge learning curve. It was kind of like realizing that you learned the alphabet incorrectly when you were little. Also I didn't have other empaths in my life, so I really had to rely on a lot of book learning and personal experimentation. It was also complicated because not only could I pick up on the energy of people around me but also of animals, of places, and even of the earth and collective humanity.

Earthquakes

One of the experiences that hit the scale of this home for me had to do with large earthquakes. My entire life, I had periods where I went from being coordinated to becoming suddenly clumsy and uncoordinated. I would get disoriented and spacey. I would do things like run into walls, stub my toe or hit my knee. In one particularly bad scenario, I dropped a bag full of plates after Thanksgiving. What a mess. I used to just think, "what is wrong with me, I am so clumsy!" Now I understand what was really going on. When I get those symptoms now, I know that I am not fully in my body. Usually this is because there is something unpleasant going on around me. It could be because of a psychic attack (more on that in the next chapter) or because I am picking up on bad energy from those around me. Either way, it isn't good. Basically, my spirit popped out of my body in order to cope with something unpleasant happening. Like any coping mechanism, it is totally understandable, but the best thing is to shift what is causing you to want to cope to begin with. In my case, these were psychic phenomenon on a really large scale so it was very hard to figure it out.

I had to learn how to shield and protect myself from intense energy, how to recognize where it was coming from, and how to either clear the energy, or get out of the environment. Depending on what the cause was, this could mean a simple change or something much grander.

So back to the earthquake. In 2009 and 2010, there were several large earthquakes. One day in Denver, I went to a museum with my good friends Sean and Sara to see the Genghis Khan exhibit. I was having one of those days where I felt really out-of-it, disoriented, tired but wired, and was having a hard time being present. As we were leaving the exhibit room, Sean called out my name because I was about to walk into a wall. Once again, I wondered what was wrong with me before trying to get oriented again. The rest of the day, I continued to feel the same way. That night I had a rough night and even though I felt exhausted, I had a hard time falling asleep which is very strange for me. In the morning, I was feeling much better and I realized there had been a large earthquake in Haiti which was a 7.0

magnitude. It is estimated that between 100,000 and 160,000 people died and the damage was catastrophic.

Still I hadn't put two and two together. It wasn't until I had moved to China and felt the same set of symptoms followed by another catastrophic earthquake that I realized there was a correlation. In February of 2010, an 8.8 magnitude earthquake hit, killing over 500 people, creating a tsunami that impacted places as far away as San Diego. Nearly a tenth of the Chilean population lost their homes and damage to fisheries was estimated at more than $66 billion. I started to notice a pattern and it was so extreme that it really made me pay attention. Now if I notice these intense symptoms, I recognize that there may be some kind of large-scale trauma coming to the earth and its inhabitants. When you think about the intense feelings coming from the earth, the natural realm, and all the people affected by these earthquakes, it makes sense that empaths could be overwhelmed with the intensity of the energies and emotions emoting from all affected by these large scale planetary changes.

The same thing happens to me not just with earth changes but also with shootings or other traumatic experiences. There were a series of shootings and terrorist attacks in the fall of 2015 which proved quite challenging for me. This included the November 13 attacks in Paris which left 130 dead and another 368 injured. Prior to that, there was a mass shooting in Oregon on a university campus and in December there was a shooting in San Bernardino. Not to mention all the intense things happening in Syria. Fall and early winter of 2015 were a very tough time for empaths.

Thankfully, I have gotten better at shielding and protecting my energy field so I am usually not as adversely affected as I used to be by these large scale earth events or traumatic events affecting people. It is possible to shield and protect yourself as well as to begin to understand why you are feeling what you are feeling. In September of 2015, I was feeling extremely heavy, exhausted and had that tired but wired and out of it feel. I got the psychic message there was a shooting coming and I even posted it on Facebook. Though it is still tough emotionally, at least I understand more why sometimes I feel the things I do.

Is it mine?

One of the biggest challenges of being an empath is determining what it is that you are feeling that is yours and what it is that is not yours. There is not an obvious way to tell, otherwise I feel I would have learned much sooner than at thirty years old that I was an empath. Since it is of critical importance to determine if something is yours or not, I have outlined some ways that can help you determine if something you are feeling is yours.

The first thing I recommend is to ask yourself if what you are feeling/sensing is yours. You may get an immediate feeling of yes or no. If not, that is ok, it is possible to do a more in depth analysis. The second question I recommend asking yourself is if there is a reason you are feeling this way? By that, I mean a concrete reason. If you are feeling sad, is it because someone just died? Did you see something sad happen? Did something sad happen to you? If there is no trigger to your emotion, it is very likely that you are picking up on an energy from something or someone else. The same is true for physical sensations. If you are feeling pain in your body for example, did you sustain an injury? Do you have chronic pain in that place? Is there any reason you can think of why that part of your body should hurt? If the answer to these questions is a no, it is highly likely that you are feeling something from someone or something else. It is also possible that you are experiencing a form of psychic attack, but I'll discuss that more in the next chapter on that specific topic.

If you are asking yourself these questions and are getting answers that indicate the source is not coming from you, the next step is to determine what the source is. As an empath, think of yourself as psychic and an energetic sponge. You absorb and take on an incredible amount of energy from people around you, from the environment, from your food, and even from energy beings that are invisible to those without psychic gifts. If you are feeling something negative, ask yourself the following questions.

- Have I been around someone or something negative?
- Is someone around me feeling this too? If so, does it seem like it was theirs first, or yours first? Are you prone to this feeling/condition?
- Did how you feel change suddenly or quickly?
- If you changed quickly, was there a change of environment or people around you?

If these questions do not provide clarity for you and there is no reason you can identify for you to feel what you are feeling, it is possible that there is a dark entity or other attachment that is around you and you are feeling the impact of its energy and influence. It is also possible that you have absorbed a lot of negative energy from something in the past and never cleared it. Let's say you were abused as a child, the energy of abuse is incredibly negative and toxic. As an empath (think psychic sponge), until you wring out the dirty water you have absorbed, you will feel heavy, dirty and just plain bad.

Once you have determined where you think the emotion or feeling is coming from, it is time to clear it. First, ask the angels to remove the source of the energy from your life. You must really mean this though. If the source of a lot of negative energy is from a boss or friend who is nasty to you, you have to be ready to let go of that person and situation or it won't do any good. If you are having a hard time letting go, ask the angels to help you release self-sabotaging behavior. Next ask the angels to help clear you of any negative energy you have absorbed. You can visualize this happening. You might also do additional things to clear your energy field like take a walk in a nice location, take a bath or shower, listen to peaceful music, etc. Then ask the angels to help fill you up with the kind of energy you'd like. You can ask for the energy of peace, love, abundance, ease, etc. Allow yourself to receive and let the angels help you. Another very helpful step for lasting change is to ask the angels to help you clear any negative patterns or behavior and replace them with habits and patterns that you would prefer. This step is so helpful if you want to make big changes fast. To recap, below are the steps I recommend to help clear and shift your energy as an empath:

- Remove the source of the energy.
- Clear the energy that you have absorbed from your energy field.
- Ask the angels to help fill you with the kind of energy you'd like instead.
- Ask the angels to help you change your pattern to a healthier pattern you would enjoy more.

This process as I've listed it is definitely simplified as there are certainly nuances. For example, if you have been in an abusive relationship for years, your energy is going to need a thorough cleaning. Asking the angels to clear you for a few minutes is likely not going to do the job. You will need to ask the angels for help and focus on this for a longer period of time to get fully cleaned up. Imagine dipping a car in tar. Simply wiping it off with a paper towel is not going to do the trick! You will need a deep and thorough cleaning and detailing to really get all that grime off. That is what being in an abusive relationship is like, it energetically coats you with nasty energy slime that is like tar and difficult to get off. It is possible, but it will take focused determination and effort by you and your angels to do it. You must also get yourself out of the environment that is causing all of the nastiness. There is no point in trying to clear yourself off if you are just going to get slimed again.

You must take a look at your belief systems. What belief or beliefs do you have that are allowing this situation in your life. Your beliefs are the root cause of just about everything in your life. Your beliefs create your pattern and together they attract people, situations, and outcomes to you. If you want to change your situation, you must examine what belief it is that you had in the first place that allowed this energy into you. These unhealthy beliefs can be rooted in current or past-life traumas or experiences. If you'd like to read more about how to shift these, you can read my book *Angels and Manifesting*. Getting at the basis for our beliefs is instrumental for shifting unhealthy patterns. In more simple cases, the process is much simpler. For example, let's say you are in line at the grocery store and encounter an individual with negative and toxic energy. You feel tired after going to the grocery store, think about it and pinpoint exactly when and where you became tired. Once you've identified the cause, ask the angels to clear you. You are no longer in the energy so there is no need to change your environment at this point. You can also ask the angels to help shift any belief that attracted you to this person and that time and vice versa. There are no accidents, so even happenstance is not random. A situation like this however, is relatively faster and easier to shift and clear than a habitual pattern of abuse.

Empaths are far more likely to be moody than non-empaths. This is because the energies and people around them are constantly changing. Remember, an empath feels whatever others feel, unless they shield from it. This means that as your environment and those around you change, so will you. I used to be described as a chameleon. That is because I naturally adapt and adjust to my environment. There are benefits to this though there are obvious challenges as well, particularly if the environment is not a positive one.

Empaths are also more likely to be chronically exhausted than non-empaths. Think again of the wet sponge. Imagine how heavy a waterlogged sponge is compared to a dry one. If you are an empath and you are filled with foreign energy, it is exhausting. You don't even have to do anything to feel completely and utterly fatigued and exhausted. Doing anything that requires any energy may feel out of the question for an empath who is overloaded with energy. There are many empaths out there who have absorbed so much foreign energy that they forget how it ever felt to be light. Luckily this can be changed! If you find that you are tired a lot and rest and relaxation aren't doing the trick, it is highly likely that you would benefit from clearing your energy field. Doing this regularly is good for everyone but is imperative for empaths.

One simple meditation to clear your energy field is to invite the angels in to assist you in the process. Visualize yourself taking an energy shower of light. Imagine that pure light energy bathing and clearing you from the outside in. The light energy goes all the way through you, purging and clearing anything that is not of the light. You may notice bits of darkness or heavy energy being cleared and released at your feet. Pay attention to what you see and then ask the angels to take it completely away so you don't reabsorb it. Do this regularly to keep yourself clean and light. We clean our bodies after all, shouldn't we clear our psychic and energetic selves as well?

As an empath, it is more important for me to pay attention to my energy surroundings than for most people. No one feels good after going to the DMV for example, or to a bad neighborhood with lots of crime, but for an empath, the experience is likely to be much stronger. Not only do empaths absorb and feel energy, but I believe that they may even have a stronger capacity for feeling than other people. Basically they are super-feelers. That means that it's extremely important for empaths to be around positive people and environments so that if they absorb energy from their surroundings, they are absorbing positive energy and not tough energy. Empaths benefit from being around people and environments that are loving, cooperative, nurturing, and supportive. Take a moment to think about the environments and relationships that you are in. What adjective would you use to describe them? If they are not positive, set intentions to release them and ask the angels to help you bring something more positive in their place.

FIVE

Psychic Attacks

Prior to being educated in psychic phenomena, I was being psychically attacked all the time but had no idea. This might also happen to you! A psychic attack is an attack that happens in the psychic or energetic realm. People can psychically attack each other. If you ever hear people talk about stabbing each other in the back, they rarely if ever mean it literally. Ghosts can also psychically attack a person (remember a ghost is just a person without a body). Energy beings that aren't and were never physical can also attack. This might mean a dark entity or a demon. When you get attacked psychically, it is often (but not always) less extreme than a physical attack. The most intense form of psychic attack would be a possession or attempted possession in which the targeted person may experience extreme physical symptoms including body changes, vomiting, and extreme pain and discomfort. Most psychic attacks are much less severe and can sometimes be so subtle that people dismiss them. Signs of psychic attack can include one or more of the following:

- Headache
- Fatigue
- Dizziness
- Brain fog
- Nausea
- Tired but wired feeling
- Clumsiness
- Unexplained pain or tenderness
- Accidents
- Negative thoughts and feelings about yourself or others

For me, one of the most common forms of psychic attack is an unexplained headache. I say unexplained because usually there is no known physical reason for it. If I was going through caffeine withdrawal or hit my head, I could expect a headache. Headaches from psychic attack have no known physical cause and usually come on quite quickly and unexpectedly. They can feel like a sharp pain or a dull throb. The reason one feels pain is that someone or something from the psychic world is affecting your energy body. We have our physical self and our energetic self. They correspond with each other and something that affects the physical body will affect our energy body. Conversely something that impacts our physical body will eventually impact our energy body as well. If our energetic body is attacked, we can feel it physically. When you get a headache because of psychic attack, something or someone is either damaging your energetic mind or inserting itself and trying to manipulate. For example, a dark entity might be intruding into your mind to implant foreign ideas. This will feel painful and unpleasant. Imagine someone putting a probe into your brain, it would not feel good.

Another sign of psychic attack is fatigue. When you are feeling energized and suddenly feel exhausted, that is often a sign of psychic attack. This is happening because something or someone is syphoning off your energy. This could be an energy being that is attached to your energy body and is literally draining you like a leech. It could also be from a person who has created an energy cord (a psychic energy connection between the two of you) through which energy and information flow. For example, if there is someone you know who feels like a victim and is always taking energy, an energy cord can be established. Sometimes we call these people energy vampires. This is not to be confused with real vampires that consume energy or blood. When we feel sudden and instant fatigue like this, we can ask the angels to clear whatever is causing the fatigue and take it away from us permanently. We can then ask for help healing and for more energy. The angels can give you a sort of energy transfusion to help boost your energy from the energy that you lost.

Another big sign of psychic attack is dizziness. This happens when something traumatic is happening to our body and our spirit is popping out of our body as a coping mechanism. We get dizzy because we are not grounded in our body. We are floating above and feeling a sort of vertigo as a result. When we feel dizzy like this, we must clear whatever is causing us to feel dizzy so that we can feel comfortable in our body again and return to it. In the case of the feelings I had prior to the earthquake, this was due to me picking up on feelings empathically from the earth and its inhabitants, almost like the earth feeling queasy prior to vomiting. I was feeling it too. This can also happen as a result of a psychic attack when a being or person purposely sends you negative energy which causes you to vacate as a coping mechanism. Not only does this not feel good but also makes you less effective because you are not completely present in your physical body. This can lead to injury and ineffectiveness and inefficiency with tasks.

Related to dizziness is a feeling of brain fog. If you are having a hard time thinking or concentrating, it could be because there is something in your energy field and you are popping out of your body, making it tough to connect with your brain and process. It could also be because there is foreign energy in your mind, jamming your thought processes. Either way, it's bad. If you are experiencing brain fog, ask the angels to clear whatever is causing it and help you heal. You can get brain fog from environmental factors as an empath or you can feel it because something is purposefully attacking you.

If you feel nauseated, it can be because there is invasive and foreign energy in your energy field. This could come from a ghost or an entity. A person who is very good at manipulating energy can do this too though that is less common in my experience. This foreign energy feels wrong and the nausea is a sign that something needs to be expelled. Just as you feel nauseous if you eat or drink something bad, your body feels nauseous because something unpleasant is in your body. The same thing happens energetically. If you are suddenly feeling nauseated and you didn't eat or drink something bad, it could be because there is something unpleasant in your energy field and the nausea is a sign it needs to be purged.

Feeling tired but wired is a sign of psychic attack because you can feel drained from whatever is attacking you and then, on an energy level, you get a sort of adrenaline response. It's like your spirit trying to say, "danger" so that you can take action to clear whatever it is. The problem is most people don't recognize it. Some people even take a sleeping pill when they experience this so they are even less effective and aware of what is happening and cannot protect themselves (I did this when I was with my ex-husband). If you have this feeling, ask the angels to clear what is causing your fatigue and adrenal response. Remember it can be only on a psychic level so there may be nothing in the physical realm, aside from your feeling that something is wrong.

When you are feeling clumsy, it can be because you are feeling unpleasant and have popped out of your body. This can be because of an empathic response to something around you or because of specific and purposeful attack from something around you. It is imperative that you clear whatever is attacking you if that is the cause of your clumsiness. The clumsiness is only a symptom and the cause is whatever is causing you to pop out of your body. If you have times when you are coordinated and then inexplicably, you become clumsy, this could be why. Nothing happens by chance really so we just have to figure out what the cause is, if it's not immediately apparent.

Just as if you are physically attacked, the presence of pain can be a big indicator of attack. If you feel a pain that cannot be physically explained (a headache is just one form) then you may be getting attacked in the place where you feel the pain. You might even have chronic pain in that part of your body with no known cause or it could be a one-time thing. I often have gotten attacked in my ankles or knees when dark entities are latching on, feeding on my energy, and trying to limit my mobility. Once I was beset by sudden and intense pain on the back of my left leg. I had not injured it and so the pain made no sense. Throughout the day it got worse and the next morning, I was literally limping. I finally thought to look at my leg psychically and I had a dark entity attachment that was chewing on the back of my leg. It was a real mess! I cleared the entity and the pain immediately got much better though my energy body still took some time to heal, just as your physical body does. Remember pain is not the problem, pain is a message to you that something is wrong. Too often people try to numb the pain through medication or some kind of coping mechanism without clearing the source of the pain. If you cannot find a physical source, it is likely a result of something happening in the spiritual or energetic realm.

How can you tell the difference between something that has a physical cause and something that has an energetic cause? Well the main way is to check it out and investigate. Ask yourself is there a physical source for this I can sense? Can I determine something directly or indirectly that may be creating a physical reaction? If the answer is no, then it is likely coming from the energetic or spiritual plane. Even if there is something that could be physically causing it, that doesn't mean there isn't also an energetic explanation as well. For example, if you trip and fall and hit your knee, the fall is the cause of the pain but it is possible that something caused you to trip. I have seen this over and over again. I have watched dark entities trip people and cause accidents.

Strange accidents are also a sign of attack. These accidents can be major (a large traffic accident leading to a pile-up on the highway) or they can be minor. You might be just about to leave the house and spill coffee on your dress or suit that you just picked up from the cleaners. You then get frustrated and have to find something else to wear, knowing that you will have to get the item cleaned again after not wearing it. All of this is designed to frustrate you and lower your vibration. Whatever is attacking is likely feeding on your frustration, pain, etc. The dark will also do things like this as a form of sabotage to try to get you to change your thoughts and feelings in a negative way so that you will manifest more negative things through the law of attraction.

One of the major red flags that you are being psychically attacked is negative thoughts about yourself or others. Since dark entities thrive on all things negative, there is nothing that they would like more than to cause negative feelings and dissension or even violence. These negative feelings and thoughts may be aimed at you and can include feelings of worthlessness, self-hatred, and depression. A major coup for the beings that feed on darkness is suicide. Every time someone commits suicide, the dark rejoices. When negative thoughts and feelings projected by the dark are aimed at others, the results can be catastrophic. Mass killings done by individuals are often the result of an individual being psychically attacked and influenced to plan these brutalities. The *Dark Knight Rises* shooting in Aurora, Colorado is an example of this. The shooter James Holmes killed twelve people and injured seventy at a midnight showing in Aurora, Colorado. Situations like these are enormously destructive and are a win for the dark because not only were so many people impacted directly through the attacks, but the media attention put the entire nation, and even parts of the world, in fear. If you are having negative thoughts about harming yourself or others, it is highly likely that there is a dark being planting these intentions within you. In this case, ask the angels to clear whatever is causing these negative thoughts and feelings and then ask them to clear any negative energy that the being, or beings have left behind.

How to Clear Psychic Attacks

To clear a psychic attack, the first step is to ask the angels to clear up what is causing the attack. This could mean taking away an energy being or removing psychic daggers that a live person sent your way. Either way, the important thing is to ask for the cause to be removed. There is no point in trying to heal until the cause of the problem is gone.

Once you feel the source is removed, it is important to ask for any energetic cords, residues, or attachments to also be removed. There may be an energy being who was sending you negative energy but they may have corded you as well. Even if the beings themselves are removed, you will not feel relief until energy cords and residues from them are gone also. People can get psychically slimed a la *Ghostbusters*. When this happens, they will likely feel awful until the slime is removed. I once had a reading by a psychic who did not call on protection prior to our reading (this was prior to working as a psychic myself) and after the reading I felt hopeless and suicidal and was literally sobbing. This happened quite quickly as I had been in a good mindset prior to the reading. It was not until the slime itself was removed that I was able to get relief.

Once any negative energy is removed, ask the angels to heal any negative impacts on you and fill you with healing, love and light. Just like when you sustain a physical injury, you need healing in the energetic realm as well. If you have received a massive attack, it may take you some time to heal or it may be a quick recuperation. After an attack and clearing work, I suggest to clients to get lots of sleep (the body heals itself during sleep), drink lots of water, and to only expose themselves to nice energy.

To recap, here are the simple steps to clearing a psychic attack:

- Ask the angels to heal any of the negative impacts from the attack.

- Request protection from the angels for this type of attack in the future.
- Ask the angels for help with what you'd like instead.

Why Psychic Attack Happens

Psychic attack happens for many different reasons. One of the most common is that you are in an environment or surrounded by people with a lot of dark attachments that are attacking you. If you find that this happens a lot, it is a good idea to start examining your life and looking at why you are exposed to such darkness all the time. If this is a habitual thing, it would benefit you to make changes. If the darkness comes from the environment where you work, release your job and find another. If it is coming from your family, perhaps you need space from them. If you have a friend that is negative, perhaps he or she is not truly a good friend to you. If you are habitually around negativity, then it is also important to look at your beliefs and patterns. What is it in you that is attracting, or at the very least allowing these situations? Do you believe that you can't have, or don't deserve better? Do you allow it because you value others over yourself? Are you feeling trapped in these situations because you are in fear and scared to release them? By identifying whatever the core belief is, you can more easily clear these unhealthy beliefs and replace them with beliefs that are healthier and better for you. Asking the angels to help is a great first step. There are many great tools to help you shift beliefs including reiki, tapping, NLP (neuro-linguistic programming) and more.

Another big reason for psychic attack is that you are empathic. This might seem unfair but it is just a fact that empaths are easier to impact and influence energetically than non-empaths.

Since dark beings are always looking for easy prey, empaths are a big target because the simple presence of dark beings is enough to impact the empath. Dark beings do not even have to do anything – empaths are easy pickings for them. So if you are an empath, it is especially critical that you take care around the energies, environments, and people that you expose yourself to. Learning good clearing and shielding techniques is also instrumental. Since the dark rushes in without invitation, it is also imperative to invite angels and the light into your life. Otherwise, only the dark will have a presence in your life, keeping you in struggle, pain, anxiety, sadness, etc. without the light aspects like love, joy, fun, peace, fulfillment, etc. If you are an empath being psychically attacked, follow the steps above for clearing psychic attacks. It will likely be a process of shifting and releasing unhealthy patterns and situations. I discovered I was an empath about 7 years ago and started shifting and releasing right away but the process will continue. First I had to learn not to be in really toxic environments (cheating spouse, abusive boss, etc.) and now I am continuing to release lesser damaging but still unhealthy situations and environments (those who don't honor me and my value, expecting less than I can have, sympathizing with those who are acting like victims, etc.). I believe that as an empath, when you release beliefs, environments, and relationships that allow negativity into your life, the attacks will be greatly reduced or even eliminated.

If you are a bright spirit or soul, you may also attract more than your share of attacks. The reason for this is the dark is really attracted to the light. Think of moths attracted to a lightbulb. Everything is attracted to the light but especially those that do not create their own light. This might mean that relatively weak dark entities are drawn into the light. It can also be a form of sabotage. Those that have a lot of light and have learned a lot of spiritual lessons are often teachers to other souls. This is because the process of enlightenment or ascension is literally about letting go of darkness. So as we learn, we release darkness and become points of light ourselves! The dark is quite smart and they find it much easier to attack the teacher souls or light-bearers than to attack everyone the same amount. This means that lighter souls can receive significantly more attacks than darker souls.

Once a soul has no darkness at all, they ascend into the light and the darkness can't reach them at all. The more a person clears any psychological or energetic openings for the dark, the less they can be impacted. A lot of teacher souls have learned about love and light to help others but still have to learn to include themselves in the love and light as well. Teacher souls often have to learn that they do not need to suffer in order to help those in the dark. It is possible to teach and share without being damaged or hurt. One cannot help others if one gets pulled into the darkness. On an airplane we are told to put the oxygen mask on ourselves first before helping others with theirs. So it is true in the spiritual plane. Once we stop allowing the darkness in through various emotional triggers and patterns, the attack will stop. We have to release any underlying beliefs that this type of attack is ok and clear any openings we have that allow the dark in. Openings can include trusting those who are untrustworthy, maintaining self-destructive relationships or habits, settling for anything less than what you truly want, etc. Everyone's triggers and openings are different and relate to whatever lessons the person is working on as a soul as well as past and current-life traumas.

You may also be experiencing more than typical psychic attacks if you are about to make really positive changes as a soul and the dark is trying to stop you from doing that so they can continue to feed. Let's say you have decided to stop drinking because when you drink you make poor decisions, feel sick afterwards, and are unmotivated to make change. Since drinking is a coping mechanism for many, the dark knows this and creates an especially bad day for you so that you want to turn to drink to feel better. If we really want to make change, we must work through these temptations and choose the light path anyway. Once we get over that hump, it becomes much easier. The dark knows exactly which buttons to push to keep us in our old patterns. We have to be smarter than the dark and more determined.

To recap, you may get attacked for the following reasons:

- You are in an environment or around people where there is a lot of darkness.
- You are an empath and more easily targeted by dark beings.
- You have a lot of light as a soul and attract darkness.
- You are a teacher soul and the dark is especially invested in stopping you from doing your work.
- You are about to make big positive changes or do something good and the dark is trying to sabotage it.

Regardless of the reasons, follow the steps to clearing psychic attacks and you can make major progress and prevent attacks in the future.

SIX
I Can't Eat That

As a psychic and an empath, I am way more sensitive to a lot of things than most people are. I have come to believe that the things that I am sensitive to are bad for most people but especially bad for me because I am so sensitive. I am more sensitive to certain food and drinks, and toxins than others. As a child, I was sick a lot and as an adult I struggled with allergies, recurrent sinus infections, and later with depression, polycystic ovary syndrome (PCOS), leaky gut syndrome, IBS (Irritable Bowel Syndrome), acne and skin problems, and insomnia. Interestingly, once I changed my diet, many of these problems went away and I responded much better to the treatments I was getting.

I am convinced that one of the reasons we have such a sick society is that most people are eating poorly. On top of that, people are exposed to all kinds of unhealthy toxins. No one can be truly healthy when exposed to them, but empaths or sensitive folks will have an especially hard time. In this chapter, I list the things that I am sensitive to and that other empaths I know are sensitive to. Keep in mind your list may be different than mine, but I've only included the things that seem to be problematic for a lot of people. Many of the things we have been told are healthy are actually not for a lot of people.

Caffeine

One of the first things that I released as a psychic was caffeine. When I first began doing psychic work, I knew I was addicted to caffeine, but I just couldn't seem to kick the habit. Caffeine burns your aura and makes it harder to be protected from dark energy. I asked the angels for help and though I didn't make the connection at the time, the angels purged me of the addiction. I vomited for twenty-four hours and when I stopped, I didn't even want caffeine anymore. I made myself a morning cup of coffee and realized I hadn't drunk it half-way through the morning. This was strange as I normally had 2, or even 3 cups of coffee. The next morning the same thing happened and again I was puzzled. The third morning, I made myself drink the coffee and promptly felt ill, anxious and had trouble breathing. I learned my lesson. I still like the taste of coffee and switched to decaf, but eventually I realized that even decaf was causing me problems and was part of the addictive cycle, so I gave up decaf too.

Almost our entire society is hooked on caffeine and one of the main reasons is that people are tired and unmotivated in their lives, so they are trying to fix that feeling by taking caffeine which is a stimulant. If we shift the things that are making us tired and unmotivated, that makes for a much healthier and more satisfying life. Even after we make those changes however, we may still have the addiction to this stimulant which means we will need to clear that as well. Caffeine taken over a long time creates a stress response in our body and adrenal fatigue. This means that your body's adrenal glands (the glands designed to give you a boost of energy when you are under stress) get burnt out. If you are then in a stressful environment, you no longer have any juice left in your adrenals. Just as your body is not able to physically cope, your

46

body's psychic protection (the aura) is also weakened. Additionally, many who use caffeine to perk themselves up are in a constant state of stress and if they need a boost from the body's natural body systems, they don't have it. If you are addicted to caffeine, it is probably a sign that there are some bigger issues in your life that need to be addressed, such as why are you so tired that you need a stimulant to get going? Perhaps you need a stimulant because you dread your job or because you have no excitement in your life. Taking caffeine is a coping mechanism but unfortunately, it allows a person to stay in an unhealthy pattern for longer without addressing and shifting the real problem.

I took caffeine for years because I was working jobs and hours that I didn't really love. I am very nocturnal but like most people, I took jobs and had a career path which required me to be up very early in the morning. This was unnatural for me and I struggled a lot to get going in the mornings. My body is wired to be up late and sleep late. I fought it for years and did manage to win (I thought) but unfortunately, the result was that I became more sick and depleted over time (not to mention unhappy). I also was using caffeine because I was working jobs and just generally in a career path which felt like a lot of work and a drain on me. At the time, I thought that was my only option. I know better now, of course! I bring this up because if you are addicted to caffeine and are trying to use it to cope with fatigue, stress, and lack of motivation, know that you can have better! There is no reason to have to settle in this way. Asking the angels to help you change the things that make you feel like you need caffeine and releasing your caffeine addiction itself are great steps.

Wheat and Gluten

There has been a lot of talk in the media and society about gluten and wheat and how it is tough for a lot of people to process and digest healthily. You do not have to have celiac disease in order to react poorly to wheat. Celiac disease is an autoimmune disease in which the lining of the small intestine is damaged when gluten is consumed. In my case, I do not have celiac disease and I am not medically allergic (according to the prick test anyway,) but when I have wheat, I get congested like I have a cold, my digestion is poor, and I get scabby skin rashes and break outs. Keep in mind the skin is the clearing organ for the intestines, so if you have a lot of skin problems, it is likely because your digestive system is distressed and your body is purging out the toxins through the skin. It's gross but important to know. I consulted with a naturopath and nutritionist and she immediately took me off wheat. It was rough for a while. I learned that wheat has a very high glycemic index which means it processes as sugar in the body. Basically it created a sugar addiction cycle in my body and I was a wheat addict! I worked through it though and after a few months, the cravings stopped. My skin and digestion got much better and I became less congested.

Eliminating wheat from my diet was one of the best things I think I did for my health. If you want to read a book that talks specifically about why wheat is so bad for the body, you can read the book *Wheat Belly* by Dr. William Davis who is a cardiac surgeon. This book goes into lots of details from a medical perspective about why eating wheat is not a good idea. Amongst other things, wheat causes inflammation which is one of the main sources of aging. Interestingly after I had stopped eating wheat, my feet went back to my middle school shoe size. In high school, I thought my feet had grown a shoe size, it turns out that I was just swollen! This was great because I appreciated having smaller feet, but the inflammation was decreased in the rest of my body as well, which is really good for health reasons. When we are inflamed, we are prone to disease and even cancer. In *Wheat Belly*, heart surgeon Dr. Davis discusses how when he took his patients off sugar, their diabetes and arthritis went away. They also lost weight and generally felt better. I am convinced that if people simply eliminated wheat, we'd be a much healthier people.

Sugar

Empaths are also much more sensitive to sugar than most other people. Sugar is not good for you. It spikes blood sugar, and temporarily raises your vibration or energy level, but then it drops below where it was to begin with. Sugar is a stimulant as well. Sugar is bad for our blood sugar and our brains. Sugar can cause diabetes, brain degeneration, inflammation and a whole host of other problems. If you want to learn more about sugar's effects on the body, you can read the book *Suicide by Sugar* by G.N. Jacobs and Nancy Appleton. If you want to learn more about sugar's effects on the brain, you can read the book *Grain Brain* by neurologist Dr. Perlmutter. The book addresses how too much sugar can lead to depression, Alzheimer's disease, attention deficit disorder, dementia, and other terrible diseases and disorders. Those are all very real physical disorders that cause problems with the brain and the body and drastically reduce quality of life for millions.

For those who are sensitive to energy, the effects of sugar are doubly bad because not only will you be feeling the negative physical effects but also the energy impacts are magnified. Sugar essentially raises your energy a little and then it comes crashing down after a short period of time. The energetic pattern very much mimics what happens with physical blood sugar. You can think of it as a sugar hangover. You will feel tired, cranky, low energy, wired at the same time, and have a hard time thinking. Sugar and other addictive substances are very sneaky because we associate the high we get immediately after we consume the substance with them. However, the crash is more truly reflective of the energy of the substance. If you felt like you did when the effects of sugar wear off immediately after you consumed it, you would probably not like sugar very much at all. Sugar really blocks the psychic channel as well and makes it hard for you to receive information from your angels and spirit guides. Since our guidance comes through our intuition, anything that negatively impacts our intuition has a direct negative impact on our life.

Reducing or even eliminating sugar is highly recommended for sensitive and empathic people. By the way, this includes fruit. We have been given the message that fruit is healthy, but the truth is that it is healthy in very limited amounts, ideally in whole fruit form. According to the *Bullet Proof Diet* book by Dave Asprey, no more than the amount of sugar in two small apples is healthy per day. Most people have more than this in just their morning coffee! When you juice fruit, you remove the fiber which reduces and slows down the absorption of sugar into the blood stream. If you are having fruit, consuming the entire fruit rather than juicing it is recommended. I am an advocate of juicing with non-sweet fruits and vegetables. Unfortunately, most juices sold are incredibly sweet and therefore toxic to the body and very tough for sensitives to handle because of the negative energy associated with sugar.

Personally, once I eliminated sugar, I noticed huge, positive shifts in my energy level and health. I stopped feeling tired all the time, I slept better, my allergies improved, I lost weight, and my skin cleared up. What surprised me is that I got sharper, my finances improved and I got better at manifesting too. Anything that lowers your energy negatively impacts not just your body, but all areas of your life.

Non-Nutritive Sweeteners

There is a lot of discussion about non-nutritive sweeteners out there. In my experience, most alternative health practitioners agree that artificial sweeteners such as aspartame, sucralose, acesulfame potassium, and saccharin are very toxic. I was diagnosed with hypoglycemia when I was in high school. This means that my blood sugar rises and falls way faster than most people's. I am extra sensitive to sugar. When I was diagnosed, my doctor took me off sugar and I started drinking diet soda. As a high schooler, it seemed crazy not to have some kind of soda. It didn't take long before I was hooked because artificial sweeteners are actually more addictive than sugar. I didn't know this although I did eventually figure it out. Did you also know that artificial sweeteners are a neuro-toxin and that their approval by the FDA is much contested? You can read the Huffington Post article, *The Deadly Neurotoxin Nearly EVERYONE Uses Daily*. I used to have exceptionally good memory. In high school, I could usually remember things after just taking notes in class. I would visually remember how things looked on a page, not quite photographic memory, but close. Gradually my memory got worse and worse. In college, I started to struggle with remembering things I'd learned in class. Later I would forget names and words. I was gradually able to attribute these problems to my consumption of diet soda, chewing gum, and other things with artificial sweeteners. It was subtle at first, so I didn't notice. By then I'd been consuming diet products for so long that I didn't attribute the symptoms to diet sweeteners. After more than ten years of consuming the stuff, it got pretty bad. If I had just one piece of chewing gum or used toothpaste with artificial sweetener (which most commercial toothpastes contain), I would forget a frightening amount. I also started to get stabbing headaches after consuming products with artificial sweeteners. It took me many years to make the connection.

Once I realized this problem, I still had to clear my addiction. Thankfully the angels helped me out. Remember that story I told about detoxing coffee and then not wanting it anymore? At the same time that I stopped craving coffee and caffeine, I stopped wanting artificial sweeteners. It was a big relief. Now, if I have even the tiniest of artificial sweetener, I feel it right away. There is no doubt in my mind that this stuff is basically poisonous. It disturbs me that it is in so many products that are touted as healthy, like toothpaste and yogurt. It is also highly addictive and studies have shown that people who consume diet sodas for example, actually gain weight. I always craved chocolate or French fries or something very unhealthy when I drank soda so though the calories were empty in the soda, they were never going down alone.

Many people advocate the use of stevia, xylitol, erythritol or other "natural" no or low calorie sweeteners. Unfortunately, there are still many health problems associated with them. For example, when your taste buds sense the sweet taste, your body starts to process your food as if it has sugar in it. When there is none, the adrenals are taxed and it creates a whole host of other

52

problems. I believe you cannot trick the body like that without bad results.

Granted not everyone else is going to have the same results as me but when I have stevia, xylitol, erythritol, etc., I have memory problems and get stabbing headaches and I also often have digestive distress. It feels like someone is stabbing me in the head with an icepick and I figure that can't be good. If you are having alternative sweeteners of any kind, then note that having them in very small doses is better. However, for those who are psychic and sensitive, having none is probably the best.

Alcohol

Alcohol is another substance that I had to stop consuming completely as I detoxed and became even more sensitive to energy. I used to drink a lot. I am a very extroverted person and liked to go out often, sometimes four or even five times a week. Drinking is such a part of our culture that before long I was having at least a few drinks each time. I had a high alcohol tolerance and was otherwise in good health. As my energy shifted, I started to get more and more sensitive. First I eliminated sugary liquor, then liquors or beer containing wheat and gluten. Still, drinking in relatively small amounts started to make me sick. I'd have two or three drinks and have a nasty hangover the next day whereas previously, I would have needed to have more than eight drinks to feel sick. It got to the point where even having one drink and then half a drink left me feeling sick. Also that fun feeling I had when I drank went away. I believe that this is because the energy of alcohol was now lower than my typical energy. There was no bringing me "up" through alcohol and the crashes afterwards were brutal. So I stopped drinking and haven't regretted it since.

The only challenge I have is that our society is very much structured around the consumption of alcohol. Special occasions are marked by champagne, people buy each other drinks as a gesture of goodwill, etc. I believe that a shift is sweeping across the world and that we will see fewer people drinking. For those who are sensitive, alcohol is very low energy and therefore impacts people greatly. One effect that alcohol has is to immediately reduce our ability to make decisions. It also targets memory. The scan below shows the difference between an alcoholic brain and a healthy brain.

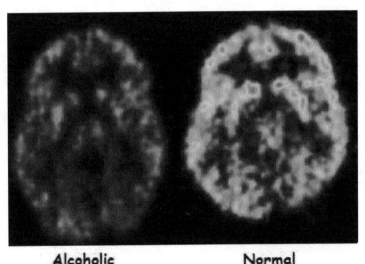

Alcoholic
Darker Colouring
indicates depressed
brain activity

Normal
Healthy levels of
brain activity

Source: wikispaces

According to the National Institute of Alcohol Abuse and Alcoholism, there are many detrimental impacts on health from drinking including:

- heart damage
- potential stroke or heart attack
- liver damage
- problems with the pancreas and potential pancreatitis
- cancer
- immune system reduction
- blackouts and memory lapses
- brain damage

The fact that surprised me the most is that the immune system can be impaired for up to twenty-four hours after drinking. Another really frightening aspect is that the more we drink, the more the decision-making part of the brain (including the part of the brain that takes care of impulse control) gets damaged. So drinking more means you make poorer decisions, not just when you are inebriated but in general. Alcohol also affects both short term and long term memory processing.

Basically all this stuff is really bad news. Even for non-psychics, the effects of alcohol are pretty nasty but for those who are sensitive the effects are even stronger. On top of all these effects, psychics, empaths, and sensitives will experience what is essentially an energy hangover. You will absorb negative energy from the alcohol and it will impact you more than non-sensitives. Unless you clear the energy you have absorbed, it will stay in your system for a long time. Remember to think of yourself as a psychic sponge. The problem is that most people drink and then they never clear their energy field from the negative impacts.

Non-Organic Food

As I became more sensitive to energy, the other things that I developed an extreme sensitivity to are pesticides, GMOs (genetically modified organisms), and irradiation. In the USA, most food has been produced with extensive pesticides, is genetically modified, and is irradiated. Unless you are buying or growing food directly from an organic farmer or you are buying USDA organic, your food is very unhealthy and low energy. Pesticides are inherently very low vibrationally as they are designed to kill indiscriminately which is negative energetically. Anything that comes into contact with pesticides dies, including the healthy bacteria in your gut. For this reason, I really struggle to eat when traveling in the United States.

The last thing I want to address here is that everyone is different. For example, my body does not process dairy or eggs well anymore. For some people, those are diet staples. It is important for people to follow what feels right for their bodies. Also note that this can change over time. One day, chocolate will feel like just what you need and then suddenly it won't any more. Honor what is right for you and your body at that time. Also, it's important to shift as you feel ready to. I didn't eliminate all of these things at the same time, it was a gradual process for me, aside from caffeine and alternative sweeteners which the angels helped me to rapidly detox from. If you want to make dietary changes, I recommend doing what feels right and working with a nutritionist who can help you figure out what works or doesn't work for you. If something doesn't feel right or resonate for you, listen to yourself. I once had an acupuncturist tell me to take a supplement and every time I took it, my stomach felt upset. I decided not to take it and later learned that I was allergic to soy which was one of the main ingredients. I do recommend doing research and checking in with holistic, nutrition experts, but only you can know what feels right for you.

SEVEN
Curses and Hexes

I debated on whether to write this chapter as my goal here is not to create a lot of fear on the topic and curses and hexes are a relatively rare thing in the bigger picture. That said, if you are affected by one, the effects can be quite extreme. My goal in discussing this topic is to help people understand what is real and what is not and how to handle it in the unfortunate circumstance that you or a loved one is being affected by one.

What is a Curse?

According to Google, a curse is, "A solemn utterance intended to invoke a supernatural power to inflict harm or punishment on someone or something." This definition reflects my experience with curses. In simple terms, a curse utilizes supernatural entities and energies to send bad luck to a person. You can think of it as the opposite of a blessing. Another way to think of it is as directing demons and dark entities to a specific person, place, or even family. While I would like to say that curses are not real, I have too much experience with them otherwise.

A hex is very similar but may imply a more ritualistic approach, though this is not necessarily always the case. According to Google, to hex is either a verb, "cast a spell on; bewitch," or a noun, "a magic spell or curse." They are in essence the same thing though different people and traditions may use them slightly differently. A person who is experienced in the occult, witchcraft, or other type of ritualistic magic may utilize curses or hexes, but even those who do not practice magic of any kind may effectively curse another as well. This is because the intent is the most important part. If there is someone who has a lot of ill-will towards you, they can curse you without any ritualistic experience or knowledge. Others, however, practice this type of magic or ritual and this may give it more power.

The strength of the curse has to do with the strength of the negative intent, the strength of the person casting the curse, the strength of any demons or dark entities being utilized or commanded for the curse, and also the strength and boundaries of the recipient. For example, if there is a weak curse sent to an individual with poor boundaries and psychic protections, the impact of the curse may be quite strong. Conversely, you can have a person with strong protections and beliefs against curses who is sent a strong curse and will be minimally affected. Each situation is quite unique. There are some people who tell me they don't believe in curses, but if they are not protected and their conviction does not go all the way to the soul level then they may still be impacted. This world is quite complex and nuanced on both the giving and the receiving end. Many souls are learning to have stronger boundaries. Those with weak boundaries against darkness are likely to trust the wrong people (they don't see the darkness in people) and conversely usually have poor energy boundaries as well. This means that they are likely to be very strongly affected in the event that someone does curse them.

The Voodoo Curse

One day I received a call on my business line from a very quiet woman asking for a healing session. In addition to working as a psychic, I am also a reiki practitioner (reiki is a form of energy healing). The client asked for a session as soon as possible. We arranged to meet the next day. When she arrived, she was very weak and actually needed help walking back to my treatment room. She was relatively young, pretty and black with a thick foreign accent. I took her back to the treatment room and was guided to give her a short reading to see what was going on before doing reiki. When I looked at her clairvoyantly, I was truly shocked at how many dark entity attachments she had! She had more attachments than I had ever seen on a client before. I started working on clearing what I saw on her and explaining what I was getting. She also explained to me that she had been very healthy a month prior and had suddenly gotten extremely sick, manifesting in all kinds of symptoms including pain, weakness, and excessive phlegm.

I did the healing for her and she noticed marked improvement after our short 30-minute session. She scheduled for the following week as well because she still had a great deal of healing to do. A week passed and when she returned she was stronger than she had been the week before but was still quite weak and sick. Once again I looked at her and saw many attachments. I explained everything I was getting while I cleared her. After several were removed, she asked me why there were so many there. I asked the angels and what they showed me

60

surprised me at the time. They showed me a voodoo doll with pins in it. I told her what I saw and she was not surprised. She asked me who did it and I described the woman I saw. My client immediately knew who the angels were showing. I described what had been done and why the woman had cursed my client. The woman was jealous and as many jealous people do, was trying to tear down my client rather than shift herself. She was also very two-faced so my client hadn't suspected anything at first. However, the more that was revealed, the more my client was confirmed what had happened. It explained the sudden onset of the illness and why she'd had difficulty healing. It also helped explain why there had been so many entity attachments feeding on my client.

After the second healing session, my client shared with me that the woman who had apparently done the curse also seemed to have a fondness for my client's partner and also owed my client money. If my client was out of the way, that would take care of both issues for her at once. Her debt could be wiped clean and the man she desired would be free. This was obviously despicable, but there are very many people with dark intent in this world. This woman had pretended to be my client's friend while trying to encroach on her relationship and making her sick with the hopes that my client would die, wiping her free of her debt and leaving her to pursue the man she wanted. I advised my client to steer clear of this woman and forget about the money owed. This woman had even offered to help my client out, all the while trying to ingratiate herself with the man she wanted to pursue. In not allowing the woman into her life, my client would strengthen her energetic boundaries against this woman. Through doing this, she would be able to truly heal. If she exposed herself to the woman who had done the curse, it would reverse the impact of the healing we had done.

This entire situation had surprised me, but I had one more surprise. As we were walking out after our second session, I asked her how she had found me as she was not within my typical client demographic. She turned to me and told me she'd had a vision of me and then searched for psychics and healers until she found my photo online. I was blown away as usually I am the one with the visions! She also said, "Thank God for you Laura." She had worried that she might die had she not gotten to the root of her illness.

This story wonderfully illustrates how our lack of protection against dark entities and curses often is a reflection of poor boundaries. Unfortunately, many light souls have to learn the hard way not to trust those they shouldn't. This is one lesson I seem to be learning over and over again in a lot of different ways. In this particular example, my client had let in a not very nice person into her home and life. She had loaned this woman money and she had not seen how dark the woman really was until something extreme happened. The less you allow dark individuals into your life, the less likely you are to be impacted by curses.

Unfortunately, many of my clients who have been the victim of curses have been cursed by the very psychics they went to. After seeing the psychic, one such client contacted me when bad things started to happen. Once I took a look and saw what was happening on an energy level, I was not surprised that the client was having a hard time. I helped her clear the dark entity that was following her and advised her to be careful and use her intuition about who to go to (reading online reviews can also provide some insight). This too is an example of having weak boundaries. We must take responsibility for the people and energies we allow into our lives. Even though there are bad people that do bad things, we cannot change them, so we must look at ourselves and do what we can do to minimize the impact these individuals will have on us.

One of the last lessons for those who are overall very light souls is to see the darkness that is there and also not to trust those who are deceptive or appear light but have darkness behind their facade. There are many who are gifted at appearing light but are filled with darkness when you look deeper. Think of a demon wearing an angel mask. It is important to look past initial appearances and see what is behind what is being presented to us.

Jealousy

Jealousy seems to be a big trigger for hexes and curses. An individual can be jealous of another's beauty, money, relationship, job, talent, or even their light. I experienced this first hand when I was performing in a show and met an out-of-town performer. He and I spoke several times and had friendly exchanges. The next day my performance partner was beset by strange sets of circumstances. Everywhere we went, people drove dangerously or swerved to hit us. It was sudden and strange and I psychically tuned in and saw that the fellow I had met had cast a hex on my performance partner. I identified what was wrong, we were able to clear the dark entity attachments that had been sent his way and clear the spell itself. Thankfully no one was hurt and we realized what had happened fairly quickly before major damage was done. In this particular case, the individual involved practiced occult magic and I was not surprised to see that he was responsible for the hex. There are times however when it is not so obvious. If there are a lot of accidents around you, strange incidents, chaos, sudden illness, depression or emotional turmoil, these can be signs that you have been hexed or cursed. Some of the signs of psychic attack will be similar. One of the reasons for the similarities is that a curse simply provides a channel for a dark entity or demon to attack. It is like a flashing light in the darkness that says, "go here."

How to Protect Yourself

One of the biggest things you can do to protect yourself is to limit exposure to dark individuals and environments. By dark, I mean dark energy. There are many places or people that appear light and bright but are filled with darkness and dark intentions. It is important to look past what people are presenting and see what they really are. We have all known people with a beautiful exterior who are ugly inside. The number one thing we can do is avoid association or connecting with those that have dark tendencies. This does not mean we should be paranoid but rather that we should take care to pay attention not only to what people are showing us but what is there. Pay attention to what people say, and what they don't say. Pay attention to what others say about them. Pay attention to their body language. If you want to learn more about how to read people's facial expressions and body language, I recommend reading the book, *What Every Body is Saying: An FBI Agent's Guide to Speed-Reading People* by Joe Navarro. Learning subtle and unconscious cues that people are constantly giving is helpful. The most important thing is to follow your intuition and follow what feels right at the moment. I also recommend the book, *The Gift of Fear* by Gavin de Becker. If something feels wrong, even if you can't put your finger on it, trust that sensation. Most of the time you will be right and your safety is more important than other peoples' feelings or politeness. This message is especially important for women as we are taught to be kind and sensitive and caring for others and often we get abused

64

because we are not watching out for ourselves and we are too trusting.

In addition to not putting yourself in dangerous or unhealthy environments, asking the angels for protection is really key. There are several angels whose specialty includes protection. One of my favorite angels for this purpose is Archangel Michael. He is excellent at protection, clearing, and enforcing boundaries. You can think of him like your knight in shining armor but with a lot more information than most knights had. Archangel Ariel whose name means *Lioness of God* is also wonderful for boundaries and protection. Think of the strength of a lion, not much is going to mess with a lion! Another great angel for protection and clearing dark energy is Archangel Chamuel. He will help clear darkness and has a wonderful cathartic and purging energy. Archangel Azrael is also incredibly powerful in terms of change and transformation. Call on him to help you release anything that is no longer healthy. Archangel Metatron assists with learning soul lessons and clearing karma. If you make the same mistake of trusting those who are untrustworthy, then he is a lovely angel to call on over and over again. He helps us integrate past life lessons and experiences and move forward. Each of these angels can help with different aspects of protecting and setting healthy boundaries.

All of these angels can help you with protection and boundaries. I recommend asking the angels to protect you every day and asking for extra protection if you are feeling fearful or insecure for whatever reason. Also ask the angels to clear any being or any energies that are not of the light and take them permanently away from you. Regularly asking for protection and making healthy decisions about whom and what you expose yourself to is what will lead you to be truly protected.

Clearing Curses

To clear the effects of a curse or hex, you must remove whatever nasty being or energy was sent your way in the curse. Depending on the strength of the one who sent it and the strength of the being or beings themselves, this may be easier or more difficult. If whatever was sent your way was minor, it may be easy to clear. If whatever was sent is bigger and "badder," then you may need to enlist assistance to help you clear it. To work on clearing whatever it is, ask the angels to clear anything any beings that are not of the light and take them permanently away from you. Ask the angels to clear any energy cords, residues, or attachments from any beings that are not of the light and take them permanently away from you as well. Finally, ask the angels for healing from any damage these beings have caused to you, your energy field, or any projects or relationships you are on or in. If you can identify who sent the curse or hex, it is advisable for you to distance yourself from the individual. Whenever possible, eliminate physical contact and ask for continued psychic protection from your spirit guides and angels.

Even though it is absolutely dark to attack another person in this way, in order to learn and shift and grow, we must always recognize our piece in the exchange. There is always something to learn from an experience. What are you being guided to learn by them? Is it to trust your intuition about people? Not to trust those who are untrustworthy? Not to automatically believe what people present to you? To be more discerning about those you expose yourself to? To protect yourself better? All of the above perhaps?

If we play the victim and don't acknowledge our part, we cannot learn and grow from experiences. When this happens, we will repeat the same lesson over and over again in this life or even in multiple lives until we do. It is much like school, you can't graduate high school if you didn't pass the 6th grade. Soul lessons must be learned in order to move forward and those we attract in our life are magically drawn to us based on what we need to learn. Once we shift, those that are drawn to us and the circumstances around us will automatically shift too. In order to change outcomes, we must change ourselves. There is no point in railing against God or the universe. We have absolute power to change and whatever we are experiencing is because there is something for us to learn from it. Those who have a hard time accepting this and are blaming others all the time are likely young souls. Have compassion for them as all souls have been young at some point.

EIGHT
All of Me

Almost everyone reading this has had many lives prior to the one they are living right now. Some have had dozens of lives while others have had hundreds. Many of us have incarnated in lives on other planets. For each life, we have had lessons we were learning as well as triumphs and traumas or challenges. Whether or not we remember them, those past lives have tremendous influence on who we are today, what our likes and dislikes are, what our blocks are, and the lessons we are learning. Often we will start to learn a lesson in one life and one of two things happen; we resist the lesson and the consequences get bigger, or we incorporate the lesson and the pattern lessens in future lives.

Have you ever felt like you were someone else or maybe like your body just doesn't quite fit who you are? This is quite common when people associate with who they have been in past lives or when they are trying on a different form to have a different or broader soul experience for the purpose of soul learning. For example, while I am definitely a woman in this life, my soul has incarnated a lot more as a man. I have a fair number of male personality traits, have been accused of being "like a man" by several ex-boyfriends, and am attracted to women. I have incarnated as a woman to have some experiences understanding and being in feminine energy for the purposes of soul growth. In many ways, how we appear in this life is like a soul costume. My soul or inner self is a warrior and I have commanded armies and ruled countries. I have a love and fascination of politics, battle strategy, weapons, and fighting that are unusual for most women. After I'd been training in martial arts for a few months, my trainer was really surprised and informed me that I did things that some of his students who had been training for ten years still didn't do. This is at least partially because I have done these things before. It is soul memory and even though I have to relearn in this life, it doesn't take long before my soul remembers and accesses the past-life knowledge in this life.

We may also feel drawn to places or periods of history that were significant for us in terms of past lives. I always had a fascination with ancient Egypt. I went as Cleopatra for Halloween when I was eight years old. I had a picture of Nefertiti in my room when I was even younger. This is not some random coincidence, this is because I have had several lives in ancient Egypt, several of which were significant lives and they really made an impression on my soul. Often the universe will literally bring us back to places where we've led significant lives in order to heal or shift something or simply to bring us into awareness of that life or even just to collect past life energy from there. For example, just after college, I had the opportunity to work in Cairo. People work in foreign countries all the time, so that doesn't necessarily sound unusual except my industry at the time was theater. I got a job in costuming and design and was an informal understudy for one of the leads in *Grease*, the musical. The odds of this being just a random occurrence are pretty slim. It is not a typical experience for a recent theater graduate to get a short term theater gig in Cairo, Egypt. Now I understand I was basically brought there by the universe to reconnect with Egypt and do some healing work.

Past life traumas can have a significant impact on a person in their current life as well. For example, if you were beheaded several times as I have been, your throat and throat chakra is likely to be weak and in need of healing. The physical damage to the body creates an energy wound as well that can only be healed in body. In my case, my throat has always been a point of weakness that resulted in me catching colds that would settle in my throat, over and over again. I frequently lost my voice as a child and this even continued into adulthood. I am working on healing the throat chakra now. The throat chakra represents communicating and speaking your truth. One of the ways I am healing that wound is by writing and speaking and expressing in other ways. Through these actions, I can find my voice and heal the wounds from past lives. If you have a weak part of your body or a body part that is prone to injury, it might be very helpful to do a past-life regression or a past-life reading and see what the past-life cause of this weakness is.

Phobias and fears are often indicators of past life trauma as well. If you have had a scary or damaging experience with someone or something in a past life, it will leave an impression on your soul and you will have fear or negative associations, even if you can't remember why. One big trigger for me in the past was sharks and drowning in the sea. I have no current life memories involving this obviously, but the thought of this terrorized me. I would have regular nightmares as a girl that I was drowning and being circled by sharks. My sister would tease me by telling me there was a shark in the pool and I would run out of the pool in panic even though this was obviously fiction (I was not living in a *James Bond* movie, after all). It really didn't matter that it wasn't real though, because the fear was just the same. You can think of it as PTSD for the soul. Once I recognized that this was a past life trauma, simply knowing that helped me clear the fear. I am not a fan of sharks, but the very thought of them doesn't strike terror in me like it used to.

In the last couple of years, I have started to get past-life flashes and insight into who I was in previous lives. There is a wealth of information in past lives, so I started reviewing past lives and gleaning helpful information from them. For example, if there was a certain person who really triggered me emotionally or pushed by buttons, so-to-speak, I would look at lives with them to see if there was anything in the past that would make the interaction have more meaning than it should. Sure enough, almost every time there was something. As is often the case for current life stuff, the argument or issue is rarely about the butter dish, or whatever it seems to be on the surface. There are often past-life grievances, hurts, and patterns that inform how you feel today. The problem is, of course, that you don't usually remember them, though oftentimes that is a blessing in disguise. It is not always helpful at first to know that someone brutally raped or murdered you in a past-life, trust me I know. On the other hand, once you do know these things, you can look at the patterns being presented to you. Everything is about patterns and healing. If you see a negative pattern with a particular soul playing out over and over again, it is always important to look at this and ask, "what is it that I am being asked to learn?" We repeat patterns until we learn why they are not good and shift to a new one. Some people will stay in a pattern a very long time, while others will shift relatively quickly. There is no right and wrong here, every soul is learning at their own pace, however, it is absolutely possible to expedite your own learning and shift towards a better and easier life by looking at past-life issues and addressing how those patterns are impacting your life now.

It is possible to look at past lives with people to see what patterns we have with them and also to look at topics of struggle or learning to gain insight. Sometimes by looking through the lens of a past life, we can gain a lot of clarity on events today. I've included some stories about various lives and lesson as examples of how these work. Of course your lessons and lives are different, but you too have patterns and lessons that you are working on learning, life-after-life.

The Need to Rescue

This need to save or rescue is a big one for me. Lifetime after lifetime, I have tried to save others from their own fate. This is very self-destructive because if someone is going through an experience for their own karma or learning, there is not much that I can do to stop it. In fact, it would be detrimental to do so. Souls learn through experience, not through someone else telling them things. When I try to rescue others, it shows a lack of understanding of their process and actually slows me and the other person or soul down. You cannot save someone from themselves. Lifetime after lifetime, this has played out for me in various ways. Often I took responsibility for something that was not mine to take and then I suffered as I took on their burdens as my own. My soul lesson is to understand that others are going through what they are going through as a result of something in them that drew the experience to them. We all are doing this and are learning different lessons at different stages. To try to stop someone from their lesson is pointless.

A lot of teacher souls make the mistake of trying to save and rescue individuals instead of understanding that they are here to help teach and share on a general level. That means that ideally, a teacher soul shouldn't be putting all of their teaching and healing efforts on one or a few souls but rather reaching large groups of people. Since we are often taught to be small and that we can't have much impact, we might make our goal smaller and focus on just those around us. This is very damaging but, as with other souls, we sometimes have to learn the hard way as well.

One of the first times this particular past-life pattern was brought into my awareness was with my ex-husband. Our relationship on the surface proved very damaging but ultimately proved to be a big catalyst for healing and understanding for me. He was someone who appeared to be very together on the surface but actually was struggling internally and had a lot of unresolved issues. Eventually those issues came to the surface and the marriage self-destructed incredibly quickly. In the aftermath, I was left wondering what went wrong. I went to a psychic who looked at the issues between us and told me that we'd had eighteen lives together and that in one life, I was a commander of an army and he was a bard (he always was a storyteller). In that life, there was a battle and he was killed and I took responsibility for it. The result of this was that when I met him again, I tried to save him. This time not from literal death, but from struggle and pain. All this did was bring about problems and pain for me as his learning had to continue and all it meant was that I was along for the ride with the struggle. Understanding why I felt so responsible for him helped me a lot to release him and let him do what he was going to do. It was incredibly freeing.

I had another ex who was also incredibly lost and sad. He struggled with depression and nothing seemed to help. I did the best I could to be there for him but eventually I realized that it was toxic for me to be around and I let him go. I later looked at a past life with him in which I came across him as a lost and sick puppy. He had a skin infection and I tried to nurse him back to health but he died anyway. In the end he died, I was sad and I contracted the skin infection that he had. It was a terrible experience for me. The dog ended up dead and I was worse for wear. By the way, I am not stating that we should not help people or animals, but it is important to note that sometimes these individuals are going through what they are going through for a learning experience and when we try to take on their burdens as our own, all that happens is we suffer for it.

Another challenging situation involved a friend who I was wanting to save from some unhealthy relationships. I was having a very hard time letting go and letting her make the choices that she was making. I asked my spirit guides to show me the life in which this pattern originated and I was shown a life in which this friend was incarnated as my baby. She got sick and I was traveling on my own and near death myself. She was very sickly and I was fairly sure she was about to die and I was on the verge of it myself. I made the choice to leave her behind. Needless to say, I was tortured about the situation. I lived and she died and I blamed myself. When I reviewed the life, I realized that this was set up karmically for her to die and nothing I could have done would have changed this. Essentially,

I was not responsible and there was no reason for me to blame myself. Just like with my ex-husband, residual guilt carried over and I felt the responsibility of trying to save my friend from bad situations. Understanding these dynamics really allowed me to let go and let her live her life the way that she wanted and needed to, not the way that I thought she should.

French Revolution

I have known for some time that I was beheaded during the French revolution. I don't know who I was, but I know I was beheaded and I knew Marie Antoinette. Recently while hosting a tour on the dark side of Paris, I received a past-life flash of who I was. I was a nobleman with dark hair and I was relatively young when I died. The information that came forward regarding that life revealed that I had been a staunch supporter of Marie Antoinette. In fact, if I had not been so vocal about my support, I likely would have lived. Just like the need to rescue, one of my lessons was not to ruin my life defending others when they had their own soul lesson to learn. In ardently defending Marie Antoinette, I did not help her but simply sealed my own fate. This was not a circumstance in which standing up for her would have changed events or changed the tide. The French aristocracy was going to come down anyway. It was just a matter of whether I was going to go down as well. Because of my decision, I went down too.

While in Paris, I also got a flash about Marie Antoinette and who else she was in other lives. It was revealed to me that she was also Lady Jane Grey and later Princess Diana. There are a remarkable number of parallels between these lives. For those who don't know, Lady Jane Grey was a queen with the shortest

English reign in history. She ruled for nine days before she was beheaded in a political move by Queen Mary. She did not even want the crown, but it is likely that her husband and her father were very much behind the move. There is a movie called *Lady Jane* starring Helena Bonham Carter and Cary Elwes you can watch if you want to learn more about her. Just like Marie Antoinette, she was executed, though Marie Antoinette had a longer rule. While Princess Diana was not beheaded, she certainly had her fair share of persecution. All three were in marriages created for the purposes of power and politics. In each life, the princess or queen was used by those around her, especially the men in her life. While Princess Diana's demise is still sad, I see a positive progression of soul learning that happened from Lady Jane Grey, to Marie Antoinette, to Princess Diana. She has learned to live longer, and better, and navigate the political terrain better with each life. She has also gotten more beloved with each life. If we all could analyze our lives in succession like this, most would likely see similar patterns of progress.

Bad Relationship Choices

Another recurring theme for me in past lives is making bad relationship choices and choosing to be in relationships which were bad for me. Oftentimes very strong attraction and being drawn together (either in a good way or a bad way) has nothing to do with chemistry and good connection so much as past life karma.

In one case, there was a man I had met and quickly we were drawn to each other. I could sense this was not a healthy connection though and asked the angels to show me a past life associated with this individual. I was shown a life in which I was married and having a very destructive affair with this man. It was not an affair about love or real connection. It left me feeling hollow and empty and it tore me up emotionally, but I couldn't seem to bring myself to end it. I recognized the same dynamics were at play. I asked the angels to clear any negative dark entities associated with that life that were still trying to influence me. Dark entities can follow the soul through incarnation after incarnation so clearing entities with various lives can be incredibly powerful and lightening to a soul. What I found fascinating was that after I did this, there was zero draw to this same fellow. I saw him for what he was, I recognized the self-destructive aspect of our connection and I wanted nothing to do with it. Interestingly after I did this, he seemed to lose interest too since he stopped messaging me. Attraction is often about learning and if one side shifts their energy, they attract a different type of partner. You can essentially demagnetize yourself to the type of partner you no longer want to connect with.

If one person shifts their energy, whatever attracted the other person has shifted too. This is a good thing though many people have stayed in marriages far longer than was healthy because one person shifted and the other didn't. There is no longer any soul learning purpose to stay together so the energy shifts accordingly. Staying in one of these relationships is like graduating from high school and then going back the next year anyway. You have already learned what was available, it is best to move on to the next phase. If there was attraction and connection and it disappeared, this can be one of the reasons why. One or both people shifted and what drew them together is no longer there.

I had a similar pattern in a life I lived in New Orleans. On a visit there I had a psychic flash about my life as a free black woman in the 1800s. I was in love with a wealthy white landowner and he was in love with me too. At the time however, cross-racial marriages were illegal in the United States and it would have made it very challenging for us to be together there. He also would have been disinherited so he chose to get married and have me as a mistress. I was his mistress for a time, but I was heartbroken and died young.

I was shown that if he had chosen me, we could have moved to France and been together and established a life together. He chose safety over me and it was devastating. This is part of the larger lesson I was living- to not choose to love those who don't love me equally or for which the love is destructive. There are those who will argue that you cannot choose who you love. I agree to a point, but is it really loving when someone doesn't reciprocate? For me, realizing this helps me to shift my feelings. I am learning to look for signs of this lack of balance in advance and release those that are negative for me early on. If I don't see this coming and the situation is toxic, at the very least I need to release the individual after it has been made apparent (like with my ex-husband).

If you are psychic, you too can look at past lives with new people you are meeting. If you are not and are still curious, seek out a reputable psychic who does past life readings and ask to be shown information on any past lives or karma you have had with the individual. It can be incredibly illuminating about the energies and dynamics at play between your souls.

NINE
Narcissists 'R Us

As a psychic, one of the things I have struggled with is the negative aspects of trying to heal someone who is hurting a lot. One type of people I have tried to heal are narcissists. The term for narcissus comes from the Greek story of Narcissus, the child of a river god and a nymph. Narcissus was very taken with himself and had disdain for others. This activity caught the attention of the god Nemesis who lured him to a pond where he was captivated by his own reflection. He was so taken with himself that he could not leave and eventually drowned.

What is a Narcissist?

According to the Mayo Clinic:

Narcissistic personality disorder is a mental disorder in which people have an inflated sense of their own importance, a deep need for admiration and a lack of empathy for others. But behind this mask of ultra-confidence lies a fragile self-esteem that's vulnerable to the slightest criticism.

The term was originally coined by Freud in his paper *On Narcissism* in 1914 and has been recognized as a disorder in the

Diagnostic and Statistical Manual of Mental Disorder by the American Psychiatric Association since 1968. Narcissist traits include:

- Being incredibly self-focused
- Problems sustaining long term relationships
- Lack of empathy
- Vanity, preening and great tendency to show off
- Flattery to those who support their perspective
- Inability to see others' perspectives
- Bragging
- Tearing down others to make themselves feel good
- A sense of entitlement
- Bad boundaries or no boundaries
- Narcissist rage (an outburst or even violence when their ego is challenged)
- Exhibitionism or the constant need to seek approval from others

There are different types of narcissists and two common types are covert versus overt narcissists. An overt narcissist is more likely to demonstrate the stereotypical narcissist traits: bragging, showing off, aggressiveness, focus on appearance etc. A covert narcissist is harder to detect (at least for me), though I am starting to recognize the pattern. A covert narcissist is highly vulnerable to introversion, sensitivity to criticism, excessive vulnerability, defensiveness, and anxiety. While these may seem very different, at their core, both types are extremely self-focused and have a very skewed perspective of themselves and other's perception of them. They also have a very difficult time seeing from anyone else's perspective. A covert narcissist can also go into a narcissist rage which gets very surprising when it pops up because suddenly you see a shift from what appeared to be a sensitive and vulnerable person to an aggressive, outright attacking person.

There is a debate on the nature of narcissism. Some, like Freud, believed a certain amount of narcissism to be healthy. Karen Horney, a German psychoanalyst and founder of feminist psychology, believed that it had more to do with the early environment a child was raised in. This resonated with me as the narcissists I have come across have usually had difficult childhoods. I believe, however, that this is a very complex issue and that it is possible that sometimes narcissism is triggered, and sometimes it is just inherent in the individual, regardless of upbringing. It can also be that whatever triggered it was in a past life and not this one at all.

According to BPD (Borderline Personality Disorder) Central, it is estimated that narcissists make up about 6 percent of the population. Amongst certain demographics, CEO's and celebrities for example, it is higher. There is actually a diagnostic test you can take online that can address where you are on the narcissist scale. If you fall into the narcissist category, it is likely that you are working on lessons of understanding and taking into account others more.

Famous Narcissists

There are many famous narcissists in the political and celebrity worlds. Here is a list of famous or infamous narcissists:

- Adolf Hitler

- Pol Pot
- Slobodan Milosovic
- Fidel Castro
- David Koresh
- Jim Jones (cult leader)
- Osama Bin Laden
- Pablo Picasso
- Donald Trump
- Lee Harvey Oswald
- Liberace
- Joseph Stalin

One reason there may be more narcissist celebrities than in other populations is that narcissists are drawn to becoming celebrities. Dr. Drew (famous for his radio show *Love Line*) did a lot of analysis on this topic in his book, *The Mirror Effect: How Celebrity Narcissism is Seducing America.* In fact, I didn't get guided to look at this topic of narcissism until it was really in my face when spending time in Los Angeles. Hollywood and the entertainment industry certainly have more than their fair share of narcissists. This was one of the reasons I started to do more research on the topic in order to help understand them better and protect myself more.

Why the Attraction

Narcissists have deep soul wounds they are trying to heal. Empaths are in their nature healers and have compassion for others. Empaths also are often overly giving and since narcissists have an incredible capacity to take, there can be a powerful attraction to each other. Since many narcissists have had trauma, the draw for an empath can be almost impossible to resist. There is so much potential for healing there! The reason these relationships are so destructive is that while an empath may learn in one life the need to have better boundaries, narcissists are usually much younger souls who have a lot more learning to do. It literally may be almost impossible for them to learn how to be nice to others that quickly. Imagine trying to teach a two-year old complex physics or calculus. It would not likely go very well. They have too much learning to do before they can comprehend these concepts. Before they can understand empathy and being kind, they likely need to have many lifetimes of incarnations to learn why being so self-focused and hurtful towards others is such a bad idea. The best thing to do is release yourself from relationships with narcissists, create distance and protect yourself as best you can. If you need legal or judicial guidance or counseling, etc. to assist you with this, then get help.

Personally, I was able to spot an overt narcissist but still struggled to spot a covert one (sometimes called closet narcissists). It was not until I realized the similar underlying pattern that I was able to spot them. Both a covert and an overt narcissist cannot comprehend how others feel or think and they are very self-focused. You will likely attract a lot of narcissists if you are in an unhealthy pattern of self-sacrifice. To make matters more complicated, I believe it is possible to be an energetic empath (meaning you absorb energy from others) but be a narcissist in the sense that you cannot see from another's perspectives. This is a mess because you are being influenced by others feelings but can only see and understand from their perspective. I write more about this in chapter eleven.

Narcissists (particular covert narcissists) may be harder to spot than overt narcissists because often times on the surface, they may appear to have things together. It is when you dig a little deeper, or look past the superficial or what they are presenting that you see the problems. Eventually, of course, they will give themselves away, but it is in your interest to spot them sooner than later. There are a lot of executives, millionaires, and celebrities that are narcissists, but that doesn't mean that they are together or doing well. Spotting and eliminating them and their influence from your life early on can save you a lot of pain and regret later.

I also want to address that though narcissists are not healthy to be around, if we find we have them in our lives, it means they have something to teach us. The universe automatically sends us whatever we need even though what we think we need may be just the opposite. What we often need is a lesson on a particular topic. Also, though narcissists often do things that are not very nice to others, they are often simply young souls acting out. Now that doesn't mean that it is ok for them to do the things they are doing, but if they are not breaking the law or hurting other people, there are limits to what we can do to stop them. If they are dangerous, then I urge you to get protection from physical resources like the police and lawyers and, by all means, ask Archangels Raphael and Michael to protect and heal you. The most important protection we have though is choosing to whom we expose ourselves to begin with. As they say, an ounce of prevention is worth a pound of cure. Learning to discern who is healthy to engage with is one of the most important tools we have to protect ourselves.

TEN
No More Self Sacrifice

It is important to know that when working with the angels, it's always a win-win. When angels help you, they don't ask for anything in return. This is directly opposite of the dark which will always ask for some kind of sacrifice in exchange. For example, if you want a career in music and ask the angels for help, they will give you guidance and assistance along the way to get you there. They are doing it out of the goodness of their own heart, they are not wanting anything in return. They feel good for helping and it is win-win. You get what you want and what makes you happy, they are fulfilled and doing their mission. Everyone wins! The dark, on the other hand, is not so generous. The dark always wants something in return. For example, if you ask the dark for a career in the music business, a contract will be drawn up, you will be asked to sign on the dotted line and you will get ten years in exchange for an early death and your soul. So it is not always that dramatic, but this does happen and even in less dramatic examples, the principles

85

are the same. Essentially with the dark there is a losing side, and something must be sacrificed in order to get what fulfills you. The truth is that it doesn't have to be that way, there doesn't have to be a losing side or a sacrifice that must be made to get the desired outcome. The dark has been on a long campaign to get people to believe otherwise, however.

This is one of my major lessons as a psychic and as a person. I have such a strong desire to help and serve and teach that I have often chosen to suffer in order to do so. In earlier lives, this often meant literal martyrdom. I died and suffered in order to help and teach. Of course, this is all very dark, even though I had the best of intentions (to help others). Since the light operates on the win-win principle, good for all, not good for some, it is important to remember that we are included in this. When we help others, not only do we not need to sacrifice ourselves, but we can actually feel good.

This is directly counter to the messages that some Christian and other religious institutions and world views teach us. The ability to receive is not the same thing as being selfish. A selfish person doesn't care what happens to others or how they feel. An evolved person finds or attracts scenarios in which they can help those who are ready to be helped and thrive by doing so. This is about caring for others as well as yourself. Self-sacrifice states that others' well-being is more important than yours or that others are more important than you are, period. Being evolved says you are important and I am important and we both matter and there is a solution that will work for both of us.

Part of the challenge of this is that there are always those who are not so balanced in their approach. If someone has a belief that they want to save and rescue those in need,

86

they will attract those who need saving and rescuing. In more simple terms, those who want to give will attract those who want to take. Each side has a lesson to learn. The giving side is there to learn that they don't have to give so much and the taking side is usually trying to learn not to take so much and how to be empowered themselves without needing others. When the over-giver shifts and starts being more balanced and incorporating their feelings into the equation, they will attract others who are similar.

All your beliefs and behavior patterns go out into the universe and draw people and circumstances to you. If you believe you need to give of yourself to others despite how you feel, you will attract those who feel disempowered and feel they need help. If, on the other hand, you believe you can help others and feel good yourself, you will attract others who are the same. Basically you will attract others who believe in win-win and then truly everyone does win.

This is very difficult sometimes because our society and many religions teach us that it is noble to give of ourselves in an unhealthy way. If we have had previous lives that were very self-focused, we may spend some time overcompensating and focusing almost completely on the well-being of others. But eventually that must stop and in order to continually evolve, we must learn and live this principle of win-win. This is the way of the light and it is the truth. There are many who are in this win-lose paradigm. They believe, for example, that there is not enough for all. In this case, that some people are the winners and some people are the losers. In a way, if that is what you believe, it is what is true because that is what you will attract to you circumstances with reflect your beliefs. Those who believe this perspective struggle with 'lack' thinking or the belief that there is not enough (food, money, joy, love, etc.) for all. These people will fight bitterly with each other for resources. There is no point in arguing with people in this mentality for they will see the world from this perspective because they are attracting experiences and people that confirm the belief.

If you want to read more about this general principle, I recommend the book *Abundance, the Future is Better Than You Think* by Peter Diamandis and Steven Kotler. They share a lot of wonderful knowledge in this book, although I disagree on their stance on GMOs. (There can still be plenty without poisoning the planet or ourselves). They site example after example of how we are now poised for all to have more than they have ever had. The media and currently held beliefs teach that there is not enough and even that many must die in order for the rest of us to survive. This is patently untrue.

Those who have learned this lesson get to the mastery level and then teach others before they ascend and stop incarnating themselves. Individuals like Oprah have learned this lesson. They give a tremendous amount but they receive a tremendous amount as well. Though people like Oprah receive tremendous amounts, they also give back tremendous amounts. There is a big difference between someone like Oprah and someone like Donald Trump, who receives a lot but does not give as much as he receives.

Right now there are many spiritual martyrs incarnated. Many people alive right now have a soul lesson not to ignore their own needs when they are teaching, helping and serving others. One way this pattern might manifest is when a person finds themselves surrounded by many very needy people all wanting help. This person could be a boss, a spouse, a child, or a friend. Or this could be a group of people or an environment for you. Perhaps you have healthy boundaries and a good giving/receiving dynamic in one area of your life, but the other areas are incredibly imbalanced. For example, your family life is alright but you are a work-a-holic and yet can't seem to get ahead. Or you have healthy work boundaries but are surrounded by lots of needy friends who always seem to need something from you.

In extreme examples, you might even be in a situation with an abusive individual. Remember that abusers are actually very damaged and hurt themselves, and are simply perpetuating this cycle. Many people are in abusive situations because on a deep, unconscious level, they are trying to heal and help that individual who is abusing them, even to their own detriment. We must remember that whatever we attract has some basis in a belief or pattern that we are in. When we release that belief or pattern, the situations associated with it will be released too and you will attract new people, situations, and environments. It happens very quickly and easily. The more you release negative, old and unhealthy beliefs and patterns, the better your life gets.

For me, this unhealthy pattern of self-sacrifice started out when I was very young, born into an abusive household. Later I had abusive jobs and bosses in which I literally made myself sick and exposed myself to toxic emotional energy because of how bad it was. Later I married a very wounded individual. I also attracted friends that needed a lot (even if it was through my energy) and then when I started my own business as a psychic, I initially attracted a lot of needy clients who were a drain on my energy. I even attracted those who felt desperate, but couldn't pay for my services.

These are all pretty extreme examples. But even as I learned this lesson, I still had remnants of self-sacrifice. I stopped the self-sacrifice on a larger scale but still gave a lot more than I received. I gave people deals on services, I had a hard time acknowledging my value and wanted to give everything away for free. I took clients where my service felt like a lot of work and I struggled with dark energy. Once I decided I was sick of that, I released a lot of those unhealthy patterns and valued myself and how I felt more. If someone needed something from me but it didn't feel good for me, I said no. It was hard at first. Any pattern we have been in for a long time will feel hard to release initially. Imagine that you have worn a rut or groove into the road and it takes a lot of effort to get out of that rut. But the more I did it, the better it felt. The lesson got more subtle after that. I no longer attracted those who couldn't pay, but they would pay, and it would still feel unpleasant. Then I released that. I realized that there is no reason that I can't feel wonderful doing work I love and provide something that others were totally appreciative of and loved to receive. This could be win-win. If you are unhappy with what you are attracting, the first step is to look at yourself. Whatever is in your life is because you allow or attract it in one way or another.

Once I shifted these beliefs, I started experiencing the wonderful things that life has to offer at even greater levels. I started traveling more; I got higher caliber and nicer clients. I released a lot of friends who were taking from me. This can be challenging; it may feel like you are losing all your friends but the truth is you have to release the old before the new will come in, not vice versa. I also literally lost weight and got healthier. I started doing many more things I enjoy like reading, writing, dancing, modeling, traveling, and having incredible adventures.

Since this particular self-sacrificing pattern can be quite sneaky, I have included several symptoms or indicators of this pattern below. If one or more of these is true for you, I highly recommend asking the angels to help you release this negative pattern and belief of self-sacrifice from your life.

- Having a job or work you don't enjoy
- Being surrounded by friends or a friend who always needs something from you
- Feeling tired or drained all the time
- Being unhealthy (you have put other peoples' needs over your physical health)
- Any kind of abuse (emotional, physical, financial, substance, etc.)
- People constantly asking you for things or support
- Feeling like you are not giving enough
- Being surrounded by toxic energy from the environment, people, or family
- Feeling unfulfilled or doing work that feels obligatory
- Receiving guilt trips from people (anyone who gives a guilt trip is a taker)
- Giving up things you enjoy because of others
- Being around people that aren't nice to you
- Being insulted by others regularly
- Receiving a lot of requests for your time, energy or resources on a regular basis

- Being in debt (you are giving more money than you are receiving)

There are many other examples but hopefully these are enough for you to recognize this in your own life and then start to shift it. When we are in a better place emotionally, physically, financially, etc., then we can help others in a healthy way. It may help you shift if you look at it that way. The more you receive, the more you can give back. The more individuals in the world live by this principle, the better everyone becomes. Think about this purely from a happiness perspective. The happier each person is the more happiness spreads. Both happiness and misery are like contagions and can spread. Which one are you passing on? The happier people there are, the more collective happiness is spread. Choose happiness for yourself and watch the world transform before your eyes. Since I have made these changes in my life, I am so much healthier and happier than I have ever been. I also regularly get messages from clients, and friends and associates about how many good things have happened as a result of my work or efforts. As I have learned this lesson, I have actually helped more and not less and you can too.

Here is a simple prayer or request for angelic assistance you can give to help you change your patterns and beliefs:

Dear angels, please help me release any self-destructive or self-sacrificing beliefs or patterns. Please also help me release any unhealthy or negative situations, relationships or habits that are holding me back. Please help me open myself to the goodness, abundance, and happiness that the world has to offer. Thank you.

You can feel free to create your own prayer as well or modify this one. Say this prayer every day for as long as you are experiencing any of the symptoms of this unhealthy pattern or belief in your life, and watch your life transform.

ELEVEN
Psychic 101

Many believe that being psychic is something that you just are. It is true that some people have much stronger gifts than others, but training and learning about psychic gifts is also key. You can compare psychic gifts to most others gifts. There are those with innate natural talent, but training can be incredibly helpful. Also psychic training and psychic concepts are not something that most people are going to be exposed to in their daily life at this time unless they actively pursue it. It's not like painting where most kids are going to have picked up a paintbrush at one point or another growing up. It is possible to live your entire life and never have tried your psychic gifts. There are those who discover how psychic they are relatively late in life. Because many psychic gifts are subtle, a person can easily dismiss some of them without understanding them for what they are.

If you want to practice your psychic senses, I've include a few psychic exercises in this chapter that you can do to practice your psychic skills. Simply put, using psychic gifts means using non-physical senses to receive information. To do this effectively, you need to be in a calm and receptive state. You also need to invoke psychic protection so that the information you are receiving is from the light. The next step is to receive the information in the way that you receive information and to trust it too. This last part is sometimes the hardest as it is easy to explain away any psychic information we do receive.

Grounding and Clearing

Before you effectively read, you must effectively clear out any psychic energy or debris that can interfere and put yourself in a calm mindset so you can receive more clearly. Recognize that throughout the day you pick up energy and information from those around you. This actually happens. You know how bloodhounds can receive an incredible amount of information with just a few sniffs? Well, energetically you are sensing stuff all day. It is important to clear out all that psychic debris so that any impressions you get energetically are from what you are enquiring about, not just who you were talking to earlier in the day or last week. You'd be surprised how much energetic gunk most people are carrying with them day to day. It can be spiritually exhausting, so that alone is one reason to clear, but most importantly we want to be as clear as possible when we read. I recommend doing a grounding and clearing exercise before reading to ensure you are clear. The grounding and clearing also helps to clear whatever is rummaging around in your mind. This is important since we receive a great deal of psychic information through thoughts and impressions.

First, I recommend asking your angels and spirit guides to assist your grounding and clearing efforts. Get in a quiet and comfy place and visualize a grounding cord going from your first chakra (base of your spine) heading deep into the earth. Visualize energy draining from your body. Ask the angels to help you release any energy that is not yours as well as any energy that is no longer for your good. Do this for as long as it feels beneficial. If you still feel that there is some sticky foreign energy, ask the angels to pour spiritual scrubbing bubbles into your crown chakra (roof of your head), let it work, and then ask the angels to flush it out. Then you want to ask the angels to fill you with light. Once again, visualize your crown being opened and beautiful light, healing energy being poured inside of you, filling you up like a container. Visualize being filled in with light from the bottom of the body upwards from the feet, up the legs, up the base of the torso, higher through the torso, into the hands and arms, the throat, up through the head, and then bubbling around the aura including above and below you. Let it fill your aura until you are completely protected.

I also recommend asking the angels to clear any beings that are not of the light and to send them into the light or back to wherever it is that they belong and permanently away from you. Ask that any foreign energies, cords, and attachments also be removed. If you feel heaviness or something unpleasant in certain parts of your body, keep asking the angels for clearing and protection until it shifts.

Angel Invocation and Protection Prayer

Asking the angels to protect you and the psychic space prior to a reading is crucial. I have known many psychics who did not do this and were fed misinformation during a reading or who were exposed to negative and toxic energies during their readings. In some cases, the client or the one being read was also exposed. In my opinion, doing a prayer of protection is not something that should ever be skipped. Reading or opening up to the psychic realm without proper protections is like playing with fire. Without knowing how to do it safely, you are very likely to get burned and have an out of control fire. If you do not do this, it is highly likely that beings of the dark will jump on the opportunity to use this open channel to send dark or destructive information.

The angels do hear our thoughts, so it is possible to do a prayer silently, but since thoughts can sometimes be muddled or unclear, I recommend doing it out loud. There are three elements that I recommend including in your protection prayer. The first is asking for protection during the reading. This helps keep out dark energies during a reading and protects you and the reading space. The second element is to ask for increased psychic abilities to turn up the volume on your psychic channel during the reading. And the third is to ask that whatever happens is for the highest good.

Angels to Call Upon for Psychic Work

Michael: Archangel or Saint Michael is a powerful protector and warrior. He is said to have led the battle against the army of fallen angels and he is often depicted in artwork slaying the devil. His name means "Power of God" and he is powerful! He can help you if you feel fearful and he can protect you against real or imagined fears. He also is great for clearing dark energies and energetic cords (energetic connections between people that transmit energies and emotions). Archangel Michael can also help you with your life mission. He is there to help many of us who have a life-purpose that involves working in the light-energy and shifting paradigms to the new way of life and business. He is also very helpful for clearing fear of any kind. He is associated with the color deep indigo or royal blue.

Raphael is an angel who helps with a whole host of issues. While he is not in the Catholic canon (approved religious text), he is mentioned in the "Book of Tobit" which is a non-canonical religious text. In this story, Raphael plays a great role in many different ways. In the "Book of Tobit", he helped heal a blind man, restored a family's fortune, played matchmaker, released demons from a young woman, and helped a traveler travel safely. This is an angel who has a great sense of humor! Call on Raphael for assistance in romance, traveling, healing, and chance meetings. His name means "Healer of God", but he doesn't heal just the physical. He is associated with the bright and deep green like you see for Saint Patrick's Day. If you find green feathers, it's probably him saying hi.

Chamuel is a multi-talented archangel who can help with romance, clearing dark and negative energy, life-purpose, and also finding lost items. He is a very powerful archangel and I call on him often. His name means "He who seeks God." Call on Archangel Chamuel for assistance with finding anything that you want in your life, including love, and clearing anything you don't want in your life such as ghost and entity attachments. He is incredible with finding lost items such as wedding rings!

Jophiel is a beautiful archangel whose name means "Beauty of God" and she does have beautiful energy! She has a more feminine energy than many of the other archangels and can help beautify or uplift anything in your life including your thoughts, emotions, your physical space, etc. She works a lot with people who do some kind of design work such as stylists, designers, decorators and artists. Call on her if you need beauty in any area of your life (even a new hairstyle!) and you may be amazed at the results. I see the color pink when she is around.

Ariel is a wonderful angel to work with for tapping into nature cycles and for working with animals. Ariel means "Lioness of God" and she is a strong force! Think of our associations with lion and you will have a sense of her – strong, dignified, and unfazed. Ariel can help us when working with the nature spirits, plants, animals, and the environment. Call on her for help in any of these areas and when you need to feel more strength and dignity, regardless of external circumstances.

Haniel can help us tap into moon energy and feminine energy and intuitive knowing. Haniel means "Glory of God" and is a powerful but gentle angel who can help with clairvoyance, divine timing and connecting with feminine energy.   Haniel is associated with the planet Venus and can also help with love, companionship and connection.

Metatron is the keeper of the Akashic Records (records of our lives as a soul) and is wonderful for help with receiving information about karmic lessons, what is for our highest good and spiritual knowledge. He is said to be the scribe of God. Because of his role with the Akashic records, he can really help us with our work on clearing karma and help us learn about our past lives.

There are many other angels that are great for psychic work too. If you feel a connection with other angels or ascended masters, then by all means invoke them in your protection prayer. You may also ask Jesus, Buddha, Mother Mary, Kwan Yin, or other ascended masters or gods and goddesses to assist you as well.

Here is a sample protection prayer I use:

"I call on my angels and guides and my client's (fill in name) angels and guides as well as Archangel Michael, Raphael, Chamuel, Jophiel, Ariel, Haniel, Azrael and Metatron to protect this space, watch over the reading, increase clairvoyance, and make sure that whatever comes through is for the highest good."

Your Psychic Gifts

So now that you have cleared your energy and invoked protection, you are ready to receive psychic impressions or information. Before we look at some psychic exercises, let's discuss how we can receive psychic information.

I've included a list of different psychic gifts:

- Clairvoyance (psychic seeing)
- Clairaudience (psychic hearing)
- Clairsentience (psychic feeling)
- Clairgustance (psychic tasting)
- Clairalience (psychic smelling)
- Claircognizance (psychic knowing)
- Psychometry (insights through touch)
- Pre-cognition (seeing the future)
- Dream walking (receiving information and conscious exploring through dreams)
- Astral travel (exploring the spiritual realm and the cosmos through spiritual travel)
- Mediumship (communicating with spirits)
- Channeling (communicating with energy beings)
- Intuition (having a feeling or sense)

When we start to receive information, it is important to note that the information can be symbolic or representative. For example, seeing or getting the impression of a stop sign could literally be about a stop sign or it could be a signal that it is time to stop something you are doing. If you are unsure, ask the guides for clarification. You will likely develop a sort of symbol language over time so that when you see something you know it means something specific, but as you are learning, it is important not to assume in order to ensure that you are interpreting correctly. The difference between a reader that is alright and great is often in the interpretation. It's as if you are playing translator from the guides to the person you are reading for so the translation step is very important. Slightly changing the interpretation can lead to very different guidance for the person you are reading for. If you are reading for yourself, the same is true!

Pay attention to everything that you are sensing once you start reading. If you have pain or tightness in a certain part of your body, that could be relevant too. Sounds that you hear or subtle emotions and impressions are all valid. I feel it's also important to not assume that something isn't important. I once was reading for a client doing mediumship and the spirit on the other side kept showing me this brilliant blue fish. It seemed so random, but I shared it with the client and she said she'd had a dream where he showed her a bright blue fish so it confirmed for her that I was communicating with her brother and also that the dream had been real. Another time I was teaching a class when one of the students was reading for another student. She said she didn't get much except she heard a loud bang. The woman we were reading for told the class that her sister, whom we had been communicating with, had been shot in the line of duty. It was clear that this was what the student was hearing. So long story short, do not assume that something is not meaningful and share what you receive. If you are unclear ask for additional insight or clarification.

I've included several psychic exercises you can do to help gain insight for yourself or others. Make sure to clear your energy field first, do your protection prayer, and then honor the impressions you receive.

Psychic Exercise Looking at Two or More Options

Get in a comfy position and ask the angels for assistance and protection. Ask the angels to clear any beings that are not of the light and to send them into the light or back to wherever it is that they belong and permanently away from you. Ask that any foreign energies, cords, and attachments also be removed. Once this is done, psychically tune into the first option you are looking at. Pay attention to any feelings, sensations, impressions, images, or thoughts you have. Do the same for second and then third or more options. Compare notes. You can do this for yourself or others. You may find that there is one clearly better or easier option and other times when that is not the case. For example, you may be trying to move or stay in the same location. When you look at moving (for yourself or the client) you feel stressed out when you psychically look at moving. You also see images of being squeezed or put in a box. Then you look at staying and it feels more easy and relaxed. You get impressions of getting things in order. That is pretty straight forward, but perhaps for another readee, you get mixed messages for each outcome. There is not always a clear answer or a black and white choice because life is gray more often than not. Sometimes the outcomes for two scenarios are mixed. If they are mixed, ask for insight as to the dynamics at play for each option. Nevertheless, this can be a great exercise to give you good insight into decisions you are trying to make.

Remote Viewing

Remote viewing is simply looking psychically at a place. Simply put, you are looking at a place remotely through your psychic senses, rather than through your physical ones. Ground and clear your energy. Invoke the angels (Michael, Raphael, Chamuel, Ariel, Haniel and others you resonate with) for protection and assistance during the exercise. Tune in to the place and see what impressions you get. These could be images, phrases, impressions, feelings, or smells. Bear in mind that what you get can be literal or symbolic or energetic also. You might see furniture or the impressions of the building or room. Again honor the details that come through.

My favorite story about remote viewing had to do with a class I was teaching. I had asked the class to do remote viewing on my home. Several students got things that made a lot of sense and then one student got information that was really different. It just so happened that my mother was taking that class and I was glad because otherwise I wouldn't have known what it was about. It turned out that the insight this particular student was getting matched my childhood home in France. I was too young when we lived there so I didn't understand that this was what this particular student was getting, however my mother chipped in and told me that what the other student was seeing was like our childhood home in France. I am glad my mother was in that class to catch it! This brings me to the point of not discounting what you get as a reader, even if the readee or client doesn't understand right away what it means. There have been many times when I have gotten something and told the client only to have them say they didn't understand it. A day or week or a month later or sometimes even years later I would get a message from client saying that what I got finally made sense so it's important not to dismiss it. The guides know what is important for the client to receive so trust that what you are getting is important. However, if you want additional information simply ask, as it is a two-way conversation. Just as with a live person, if you are unclear ask for clarification.

I have another interesting remote viewing story. When you look at a place, I find it helpful to ask for information on what is going on physically as well as energetically. During the same remote viewing exercise with the class I mentioned before, I already saw my place physically as I was already in it. I decided to look at the place energetically and what I saw amazed me. My angels and guides showed me that the energy above the living space was horrible, really nasty energy of decay and stagnation. At the time I was living in a Victorian House in the Whittier neighborhood in Denver. The home had been built in 1888 and though the home was beautiful, it had been used as a rental for many years and hadn't been maintained very well. I did the best I could to psychically clean it up, but if there is something physically wrong, then no amount of psychic effort can completely clear it. For example, I can clean the energy of the toxic waste dump, but until the toxic waste is cleaned up, it will remain pretty dirty physically. Shortly after the class where I saw how dirty the energy was above the living space, my roommates and I brought in a specialist to look at the attic as we'd been hearing noises coming from it. What he discovered was truly disgusting. Apparently there were several holes which had been allowing animals in but rather than patching the holes and catching the animals, someone had simply put down poison. Of course this was not a solution as the animals had eaten the poison and died. Then new animals came in. In a word, it was a mess. My roommates and I got our landlord to finally fix the holes and clear out the dead bodies. No wonder it had been such a mess energetically! So now when I am looking at a place and considering living there, I don't just look physically, I make sure to check the place out psychically as well.

To do remote viewing for yourself, clear your mind, invoke protection and see what you are shown. Remember to trust what you receive and know that you might be seeing something physical or energetic. Remember that what you are shown might not be obvious physically as in the example of me being shown my attic. Sometimes when we are shown psychic things, we are shown from a certain perspective. I'd like to share the old story of several blind men who are brought to an elephant and asked to describe the elephant to others. The man who grabs the tusk describes the elephant like a pipe, another feels the trunk and states that the elephant is like a branch. Another man touches the side of the elephant and says that the elephant is like a wall. Yet another touches the elephant's ear and describes the elephant as like a hand fan. In a way, this is what reading psychically can be like. Sometimes we are given a bit of information that is true but is not always representative of the whole picture. When you are looking psychically, take in what you are being shown, but remember you can also ask for other perspectives or other information for a more holistic picture.

Looking at People or Names Psychically

I find that looking at people psychically can be a very effective and helpful exercise. You can do this when you are trying to get information about someone you don't know. For example, perhaps you are trying to choose a doctor or a teacher or school and you only have their name to go by. Ground and clear your energy, ask for protection and then take a moment to get impressions of the different names you are considering. I used this when I was choosing a TEFL (Teaching English as a Second Language) school in Barcelona. There were 13 schools that I found online. If I'd tried to choose a school by logic alone, it would have been very difficult and time consuming to make a decision. I also would only have been including physical information and not the invaluable psychic insights that are so helpful. When you look at each person or name, notice any impressions you get, how you feel, what you see etc. By doing this, I was able to quickly and easily select a school in Barcelona. I selected the one I did because it felt much lighter and more fun than the others. There were many schools which felt heavy, intense or otherwise uncomfortable so it was easy to eliminate them. There were a few that felt better and one that was obviously much better than the others. I made my choice and it did prove to be a great school for me. We must remember that many things happen as the result of one decision. For example, because of the school I chose, I also ended up rooming with particular people and meeting specific people socially, so it isn't always about the specific decision at hand because the angels can see all these things even if we can't.

I also use this technique if I want to find out more information on someone I am considering being friends with or dating. The information that can be shown is often very illuminating! I once looked psychically at a magician who was flirting with me to see if I wanted to date him. He was quite funny and charming in person but when I looked at him psychically, he looked like a big mealy worm. After I saw that, I thought, "Ha ha, thank you, but no thank you!" I think this is very important to do, as people in our society often show us masks instead of their true faces. Most of us wear masks to a degree. If you want to learn more about how to look at physical cues to see what is really going on with people, I recommend the book, *What Every BODY is Saying* by Joe Navarro, a former FBI agent who uses non-verbal cues to crack cases. I recommend paying attention to physical cues and then using psychic information for the best complete picture. I have actually used the information I found in this book to pick up on unconscious reactions I was having to other people. For example, we naturally turn our feet towards people or situations we like and away from those we don't. After reading the book, I found myself noticing when my feet were turned away from a person and then checking out psychically to see what it was that was triggering me if it wasn't obvious.

Health reading

It is also possible to receive information about health for yourself or others. Keep in mind you may be shown physical things, what is going on energetically, or tips on how to be healthier. If you are getting information and you are unsure what it means, ask the angels for clarification and see what comes forward. Once I was giving a reading to a client when she asked about the health of her mother. I saw a lot of dark energy around the chest area of her mother. I relayed what I saw to the client and she shrugged and said it didn't mean anything to her. She'd apparently asked about her mother's health because her mother had recently been diagnosed with a brain aneurysm, an expanded blood vessel which can rupture and cause death or brain damage. Many brain aneurysms are stable, but when they are discovered in a person, it is often unknown whether they are stable or not. In this case, the brain aneurysm proved quite stable as it did not rupture. Two years after the reading, I was contacted by my client. She informed me that what I had seen in the reading took a while to become clear. Her mother had been diagnosed with an aggressive form of cancer (advanced metastatic melanoma) in the heart, sternum and lungs. Though the dark energy around her mother's chest didn't mean much at the time, it became clear later once her mother was diagnosed. I believe that all physical illnesses manifest first energetically and then manifest into the physical over time, so just because something is not confirmed physically, does not mean it isn't real.

I also believe that we have the ability to experience miracle healing. Once we acknowledge what is going on, it may be possible to heal from it. It is also important to understand that some people are going through illness or even death for purposes of karmic or spiritual learning. It may be a part of one's path to die in a certain way at a certain time and it is important for us as readers not to try to heal or fix everyone, as in some cases, that would be counter to that individual's highest path. If we are looking at health for a client, make sure that we are relaying information that is for the client's highest good. As a reader, we are not God and we have to understand that our ability to help a client is impacted by what that client came here to learn and experience for themselves. One trap that many readers get sucked into is that of trying to be everyone's savior. That is exhausting and it is too much pressure to put on oneself. Also if you prefer not to look at a particular type of reading, it is ok not to. While I do health readings, it is not my specialty and there are plenty of medical mediums who focus on just that. I do think that when you are learning though, it can be helpful to try different kinds of readings and see what you like afterwards. You might be surprised what kind of reading you actually like to do.

Channeling

Channeling is simply receiving psychic information from spiritual beings. These beings could be spirits or they could be gods or goddesses or faeries or angels. Some people are said to channel Extra Terrestrials. The same reading principles apply for channeling as for other reading types. Invoke protection, ground and clear your energy, and invite a being who is of the light to step forward and communicate. You can also invite someone specific to talk

108

with you. As you go through the channeling, you can ask them to share information with you or you can ask them questions. Of course they will only answer the questions they want to. I love channeling angels and god beings. Some of my favorite channeling sessions have been with Zeus and with the Archangels Michael and Jophiel. You can ask them information about yourself or about life and humanity, the world, or the universe. Sometimes I like to channel just for fun or if I am feeling stuck or can use a different perspective.

Here is a channeled message from Archangel Jophiel for you right now:

> Be easy on yourself. It is easy to push and get frustrated. Too often, humans are making progress and good things are happening but they get frustrated because they feel things should be happening faster. By doing this they are not focusing with love and gratitude on the things that have happened so far. There is no need to force or push for things to happen. You are loved and supported. Ask us to help you ease your burdens. Enjoy life, enjoy the little things. Dream big and believe that the wonderful things you envision can come into being. The angels love you very much!

For a different perspective, I also called on Zeus to share a message with you:

> You are powerful creators. Many humans mistakenly believe that you are like a leaf being pushed along in the river. You have great powers, more power than you realize. Yes, you do not need to force things to happen, but know

that you have an incredible power and will inside of you.
Allow the universe to help you but know that you are not
powerless. If you understood the power at your fingertips,
you would be awed by what is possible. Do not let society or
political leaders tell you how you can live or what you can
do. Only you can limit yourself. Focus on what you would
like to happen and let the universe and the spiritual realm
help you create it. You can call on me as well. Humanity is
in an incredible time of transition. Do not feel helpless. One
person has the ability to change the entire world.

For these channelings, I did what is called automatic writing. Automatic writing is when you simply let spiritual beings write for you. I let them use me to write. But you can also use other gifts like clairvoyance, clairaudience, or empathy to receive insight or channeled information from beings of light. Remember that there are many dimensions and many types of spiritual beings. Just because a being is not here in our physical plane, does not mean that they are not real and do not have helpful information to provide. Some of my favorite channeling sessions for clients involved unicorn or faerie guides. Honor what you receive, even if the beings communicating with you are not recognized as "real" by our society.

Mediumship

Mediumship is simply receiving channeled information specifically from a spirit in the light. I classify this differently than communicating with a ghost which I classify as paranormal communication. A ghost does not have information about the bigger picture since they only have access to the information from their current incarnation. Once a spirit has crossed into the light, they do a life review, and have a more comprehensive picture of the other side. While it can be very interesting to communicate with ghosts, I do not recommend asking them for guidance or advice. A spirit in the light is able to provide a better perspective. Still, it's important to take into account the level of spiritual development of the spirit. A very young soul is still learning early lessons so I wouldn't recommend asking for guidance from them. If you call on a spirit for guidance, think about whether they are qualified to advise in the area you are inquiring about. You can also call on spirits on the other side to catch up or say hello. Many people hire me to just check in on their loved ones on the other side. You can also ask loved ones on the other side if you want their input or clarification on things involving them or their family. I have had many mediumship clients who ask me about crimes involving their loved ones who are now on the other side.

One of my favorite mediumship memories involved a client who asked me to communicate with her mother on the other side. She came forward right away and the client asked if her mother had a message for her. I think my client was expecting something profound or deeply meaningful but her mother simply said, "tell her not to give away my fur coat." When I relayed this message, her daughter laughed and said," that is exactly what she would say". Keep in mind that the sense of separation with those on the other side is often one-sided. We feel their loss, but they come and check in on us regularly so they may not miss us as much as we miss them. They still come and hang around us a lot, even if we can't sense them. I was rather surprised to learn when I started this work just how watched we are in our daily lives. Any sense of privacy you have in the spiritual realm is really an illusion. On the other side, there is also no embarrassment or shame so it does take away the need for privacy in a lot of areas. Still if you want privacy at certain times or places, you'd best ask for it.

A few of my favorite spirits I love to communicate with are Marilyn Monroe and Michael Jackson. I've included a channeled message from each one here for you. Just now Frank Sinatra also chimed in saying he wants to talk so I will include a message from him as well.

Here is a message from the lovely Marilyn Monroe:

Hello sweethearts. I love you all so much. Too many of us think we are small. There are so many small minded people in the world and rather than being big and beautiful, we shrink to make ourselves feel better. Do not do this. If people cannot accept our beauty and power, let them go so that you have room in your life for those who can. This was a mistake I made many times, I held onto those who felt small around me. Power, money, and fame are overrated. Do not seek these things for validation, simply be the wonderful and incredible person that you are and you will attract all the good things life has to offer. I am here for you. Sending you all my love.

I love communicating with Marilyn. She has such a loving, positive and sweet energy. She is very pure and selfless. She wants very much to help many of us, particularly women, during this time when humanity is learning to understand and embrace the feminine.

Michael Jackson is also trying to help us right now and is acting as a spirit guide to many of us who are incarnated right now:

I am learning the lesson that many others are learning right now, not to trust those who are untrustworthy. There are many people in power in Hollywood and in politics who are incredibly deceptive and wear a mask so we do not see the true monsters they are. It is important to be loving, but be careful not to trust the monsters wearing beautiful masks, there are so many of these people right now. Pay attention to the energy and emotions coming from people. Do not trust those who are cold or unemotional. They will try to use logic to appeal to you. What they say may make sense but that does not mean it is right. Trust your heart.

And lastly here is a message from Frank Sinatra:

There are so many people living their lives based on the practical. What do you love? Do that! If you do, the world will be presented to you. As the song goes, "I've got the world on a string." This is what happens when you live your life according to your love and your passions. This idea that we all have to work and pay our dues isn't true. Do what you came here to do! Be big, be bold, enjoy and live your life. The most powerful thing is the power of influence and when you are in love with your life, you have incredible influence on the world. Do what you love!

As you can see each spirit has such a different message! You can ask them for help with your life or for humanity or just to see what they want to share. If you are doing mediumship, do your prayer of protection, clear your energy and see who steps forward or invite someone to communicate. You might be surprised who steps forward!

Divination

Here are some other activities that use psychic abilities: divination techniques including tarot or oracle cards, I-Ching, runes, coffee or tea leaf reading, and palm reading. In each form of the divination, the reader uses the tool to access divine information. The best readers use their intuition in conjunction with whatever the divination tool shows. For example, though there is clear symbolism in tarot cards, a good reader will be able to identify what the cards mean in relation to specific aspects of that person's life by using their intuition. So even if you do not feel you are clairvoyant or overtly psychic, that doesn't mean that you can't use one of the many tools out there to give yourself psychic information. Pick a divination method that is the most appealing to you, learn about it and give it a go!

While there are many lovely divination methods, I do want to take a moment to warn against Ouija boards. The Ouija board is a game with a planchette and an alphabet designed to provide a medium for easy communication with spirits. As with any open channel that is not protected, the Ouija board can be dangerous. I do not recommend using them unless you really know what you are doing and how to invoke proper protection. Because the intention of the inventor of the Ouija board does not feel particularly light, even with protection, I do not recommend it. The information that comes through a particular avenue will only be as light as the avenue itself. For example, I would not expect light information to come through a reader that has large demon attachments.

Since the intention behind the creation of the Ouija board is mixed at best, many dark things often come through the channel. I knew a man who once made a deal with a very powerful demon. The initial contact and communication was through a Ouija board. Of course the game cannot be blamed for this, but it provides easy access to many people who are just looking for fun and have not set intentions or set protections to prevent dark beings from coming through. I certainly would not recommend it for children and even adults should play with care.

A client told me a story about playing with a Ouija board when she was young. She was told by her grandmother and one other individual that bad things were coming through the board. She had not told them she was using the board but the family is very psychic. Her grandmother told her to, "stay away from that Ouija board, things have been following you home." Neither her grandmother nor the other person knew she had been using the board. That was enough to get her to stop using it. The dark is constantly looking for access to unsuspecting people and a Ouija board can be a perfect opportunity.

Accessing Your Inner Psychic

Everyone has a psychic rock star inside. Not everyone wants to be a professional psychic like me, but learning to access your gifts, whatever they are, is a great way to tap into the universal knowledge available to all of us and make your life and the world better. There is literally no area where psychic tools can't be helpful! Want to know who to date and who not to date? What to eat? Where to move? Where to go to lunch? Why you can't lose that last 10 pounds? Psychic insight can provide valuable information in all of these areas as well help you feel empowered and connected. Start exploring your psychic gifts (in a safe way) and watch the magic unfold!

TWELVE
Up, Up, And Away

In this chapter I will share funny stories that are unique to the psychic lifestyle. Things that happen to me do not happen to other people, so I thought it would be fun to share them here. Life for me is different than life for almost anybody else because of my gifts. I wouldn't change it, but it does make life interesting to say the least!

Your Demons Are Bothering Me

I was on my way to Paris to do a tour of *The Dark Side of Paris* and was waiting at JFK on a layover. The terminal I was in was relatively quiet and I went and found a table in a relatively calm area to read and relax before my flight. Shortly after sitting down, a woman came and sat at the table directly next to me. Keep in mind there were lots of empty tables in the area. In fact, only one other table was occupied near me so it was odd. Social norms dictate that you leave an empty seat or table most of the time. So this woman sat right next to me and I very quickly learned why. It was because she had lots of demon and dark entity attachments and they started to bother and attack me right away.

This can happen for two reasons; it can happen because they are simply drawn by my light and want to help or are seeking attention. This is much like the little boy in school who throws rocks at the little girl because he likes her. This is not a very good tactic in my opinion, but it happens a lot more than you might think! The dark is often very attracted to the light, after all, who needs the light more than the dark itself? The other reason the dark might attack something or someone light is because they truly hate or fear the light. Either way, it's annoying.

As part of my gift, I can either cross the dark entities or set-up extra shields and protections to keep them at bay. I now know though that they are a lot more likely to attack me if I have some kind of belief system which allows for them to attack. For example, it is quite possible if your beliefs, patterns, and protections are quite strong to walk into a very dark place and come out unharmed. However, if you have any beliefs or patterns that either welcome the darkness or want to save souls from it, it is a lot more likely that you will end up attacked or drained or worse. Since I was still learning this, I ended up crossing the woman's entity attachments and moving only to have another person with dark entity attachments sit very close to me. It was maddening!

When this sort of thing repeatedly happened to me, I would sometimes get frustrated and want to tell the person to sit elsewhere because their demons were bothering me, but I

118

realized that saying something like this would probably do more harm than good and also would likely lead them to think I was a crazy lady! I would have fantasies of telling the person, "Your demon attachments are really bothering me, can you please go somewhere else!" Once I learned that there was a pattern here that I needed to shift, it really helped me a lot. Once I understood why this was happening, I could figure out the underlying belief or pattern, work on shifting it and stop those people (and their attachments) from being drawn to me in the first place.

This has plagued me all my life, even when I was psychically shut down and trying to ignore all that psychic business. I will never forget the time I went to see the *The Cable Guy* with Jim Carrey at the movie theater and right up until about 5 minutes before the movie was to start, my sister and I were the only people in the theater. Then right as the previews were starting, a man came and sat directly next to me. It was so odd. There were probably about 200 seats in the theater and out of the 198 free, he sat directly next to me. I excused myself to go to the bathroom, and then sat on the other side of my sister.

I also have often been in crowd situations where people are constantly bumping into me. I will move and the crowd will follow. It was so extreme that others around me would often comment on it. Most people are doing this very unconsciously and are either being influenced by attachments who are trying to connect or bother me, or they are looking for light or help directly. It took me many years to realize that I had a lot of unhealthy beliefs that caused me to give a lot of energy and support to others. This meant that I drew a lot of people who wanted to take from me. The natural match for someone who

119

over-gives, is someone who over-takes. As tempting as it was to get frustrated at others who were trying to take from me, the truth is, I had to look at why those people were being attracted to me in the first place. Only when we acknowledge our piece in it, can we truly shift, change and grow.

After spending time and focus on shifting and clearing this unhealthy pattern, this happens a lot less than it used to! I have shifted this by doing lots of past life reviews. It is possible to look at past life patterns and note the unhealthy behaviors. Often times just by seeing how they have manifested over and over again in past lives, you can see how they are doing so in this life as well and spot similar dynamics and then change your behavior. The universe is much like a Netflix queue. When you watch movies, the Netflix software recognizes similar movies to the one you watched and suggests them. It's like that in real life. Whatever you say yes to sends a message to the universe that says, "more like this please". When one says no to a suggestion, the software notices and modifies the algorithm to send more of what it thinks we like. In order to change what we are presented, we have to change what we are choosing. So in my case, I had to stop choosing to save or rescue those who were choosing the dark either consciously, or unconsciously. Once I figured this out, that pattern manifested a lot less frequently for me.

One of the specific beliefs I had to release was that it's ok to give just a little bit to a lot of people. Let's say you have 100 cookies, it doesn't matter if you give them all to one person or 1 to 100 people, the results are the same, you have no cookies for you in the end. That is essentially what I was doing. I was giving away all my energy to others. Once I worked on shifting that unhealthy belief system, I stopped having as many people connecting with me consciously or unconsciously who were wanting my cookies, so to speak. Everyone gets their own cookies, so there is no need for me to give mine away. If you find yourself always feeling depleted or surrounded by people who are looking for help, practice saying no and holding onto what's yours.

Excuse Me, Do You Smell/See/Hear That?

One of the challenging aspects of being psychic is I can't always tell what is a physical phenomenon and what's psychic. This has led me to often ask others around me if they see or hear something. The more practice I get using my gifts, the better at differentiating I get, but it's still a challenge at times.

I was once at a nightclub to see a friend of mine who was deejaying that evening. The club was called the Funky Buddha and there was an upstairs and a downstairs dancing floor and seating area. I was upstairs sitting on a sofa just listening to music, waiting for my friend to get done with his set downstairs. A man came and sat next to me and he asked me what time it was. I looked at my phone and it was exactly midnight. I told him that and he smiled at me and thanked me, but there was something about his expression which was funny, like there was a joke of some kind and I wasn't in on it. We chitchatted a little bit and then my friend walked upstairs, so I excused myself and went to say hi.

After greeting each other, we went downstairs but something about the interaction with the man upstairs was bothering me. I waited for him to come downstairs. There is only one staircase from the upstairs area and I was standing right next to it. He did not come down and I decided to go upstairs and look for him. He was nowhere to be found. This confirmed my suspicions that he was not a live, physical person. I asked my deejay friend if I'd been by myself when he saw me upstairs and he told me I had been sitting by myself. I now believe that this was a ghost I was talking to who knew he was dead and was playing with me a little bit. No harm was done, but now when I have a strange feeling like that, I pay attention.

On another occasion, I was walking with my boyfriend at the time. We were outside on a nice summer day at *Festival of Faerie* in Lafayette, Colorado, my hometown. It was a beautiful day and there were nice foods and treats being vended and people were dressed up in their faerie finest. It was a fun event and people were in good spirits, in a celebratory and whimsical mood. As my boyfriend and I were walking, we suddenly smelled an awful stench. It smelled like rotting or death. It was horrid and really strong. He asked me if I smelled it first and I sure did. We asked a couple of others but they did not smell it and believe me, if it was physical they would have because it was overwhelming! My boyfriend was also quite psychic and those who are psychic will often be drawn to other psychic people so most of my friends are psychic, whether or not they acknowledge it.

In this case, the source of the god-awful smell was a dark entity that fed on decaying energy. Why it showed up there I am not sure, but I asked the angels to clear it and the smell went away. If there is ever a smell that seems to have no physical source, it is likely to be from something spiritual or energetic. If the smell is good, it may be from something friendly though not necessarily. If it smells bad, it is likely something not friendly. The one gray area is ghosts. A ghost may smell like they did when they were alive. They could smell like a perfume, freshly baked cookies or like cigars or cigarettes if they smoked. You can have a ghost that smells like lovely perfume but is angry and territorial but, most of the time, good smell equals a nice presence and bad smells mean something that is malevolent or at least not happy.

Once I was on a paranormal investigation and at a bar in Cheyenne, Wyoming. The bar had previously been a speakeasy and later, a hotel and then a retirement home. This meant there was a lot of activity. Bars, hotels, and retirement homes all create and draw a lot of activity for different reasons. Bars draw a lot of spirit and entity activity because a lot of people drown their sorrows through drinking. Also, when we drink we are psychically opened and anything or anyone that wants to invade or attack us physically or psychically is able to. Hotels draw spirit activity because there are more people coming in and out, bringing their attachments and energies into one place. Additionally, when people are traveling, they often misbehave, are lonely, drink more, have lots of sex or even hire prostitutes, all of which can attract or create more activity. Retirement homes, for fairly obvious reasons, have more people checking out of the physical realm than most places and when those spirits don't cross into the light, they become earthbound and often stay where they died.

This bar and former hotel and retirement home was teeming with activity! Right away our EMF (electro-magnetic frequency detectors) were going crazy and I was sensing a ton of activity around us. After doing some checking on the ground floor, we got into the elevator and I immediately got the strong scent of a floral perfume. It was so strong that I leaned over and smelled the male investigator standing in the elevator next to me. He was a very masculine guy and he definitely did not smell like flowers! I tuned in psychically and saw a turn of the century woman with dark hair. If I could have imagined a perfume that suited her, it would have been the one I smelled. The psychic scents we get really do give us insight into the personality of the origin of the scent.

The Ghost Party

I have done quite a bit of work with paranormal investigators and I was on one such investigation when I experienced a party like no other. I was with *Altitude Paranormal Group*, a Denver-based paranormal investigation group in Biloxi, Mississippi. We were doing several investigations on the Gulf Coast and for this particular investigation we were at the Beauvoir Mansion, the former home of the Confederate President Jefferson Davis. This venue is now a museum, and given its significance historically in relation to the Civil War, it is not surprising that there were a lot of ghosts there. We had found so much evidence that it really was pretty incredible. We captured the voice of a little girl that I was speaking to and witnessed objects being moved by spirits, strange mechanical malfunctions, and many extreme manifestations of spirit activity.

This investigation was a bit unusual because we were actually staying on site in one of the cottages. This meant that during the most active part of the night, we were trying to sleep in the middle of it all. In many ways, the nighttime is when spirits are the most awake or active. That is one reason why I am very nocturnal, it is typical for me to go to sleep between 3 and 5 in the morning. Oftentimes, if I go to sleep earlier and I am in a place with a lot of spirit activity, I will have restless sleep. Imagine trying to sleep when there are a lot of people talking and moving around you.

We had completed our investigation and it was around four in the morning. I was sharing a queen-sized bed with Michelle, another investigator. As I was trying to drift off to sleep, I was distracted by loud party sounds. It was so clear that it took me a minute to realize that these weren't live parties but the spirit variety. It is between the sleep and dream state that our psychic senses are often the most attuned. I could clearly hear people laughing and talking, what sounded like drinks clinking, dancing and music playing. If they had been alive, I would have been tempted to join them as it sounded like they were having a good time! Michelle, the investigator, was quite psychic herself so I asked if she heard them. She too was near sleep but after listening for a moment she confirmed that she heard them too. It's always fun for me when others perceive things from the spirit realm. It was actually pretty fun to listen to them having a good time. Not all ghosts are ever in such a festive mood but I rather enjoyed that they were having a good time despite their ghostly status. We continued to listen to them and the sounds did eventually fade away and then we were able to sleep peacefully.

These cottages are available to rent if you ever want to go and see if you can experience any paranormal activity at this most haunted location. Go to www.beauvoir.org. If witnessing paranormal or supernatural activity is an interest of yours, then I highly recommend the Gulf Coast. It is teeming with paranormal activity. You don't even have to seek it out. There is so much around, it is likely to find you. Be careful though, the living are the ones that you might want to watch out for. Many of the tours in New Orleans love to tell you that the city has the highest missing persons' statistics in the nation and that is saying something considering the relatively small population of the city.

The Fallen Angel

There are many different types of souls out there. There are human souls, animal souls, faerie souls, extraterrestrial souls, and angel souls. It is possible for one type of soul to incarnate in another form. A faerie can incarnate as a human or a human soul can incarnate as an animal to experience that form and gain a better understanding that can only be gleaned through life experience. The majority of the souls in human bodies are human but there are many other types of souls here too. There are many angels incarnated as humans right now to help us out with the consciousness shift we are going through on this planet. I have an angel soul. I've had a lot of human lives but my soul type is angel. If you want to read more about this, you can read Doreen Virtue's book *Earth Angels*.

My whole life people have called me 'angel'; some people say I look like an angel too. I never thought much of it until I opened up my psychic gifts and started to learn from others about this concept. When I read about incarnated angels, I recognized myself in their described characteristics right away. Incarnated angels are often the over-helpers. We help to a fault; we help to a degree that is often damaging to ourselves. We are made to help, after all. Angels are very psychic and my soul heritage is one of the reasons that my psychic gifts are so strong. It is also why I can see some of the realms that some other psychics do not see. I can see demons, dark entities, and angels with clarity that is unusual and that is because basically those beings are of my realm. Now most angels out there are of the light, but angels have freewill and can fall into the dark as well. Because they are so powerful, when they do, the effects can be quite devastating. Some fallen angels never come into the light again but some of them realize their errors and are trying to return to the light. When this happens, they have much learning and karma to clear in order to accomplish this.

One day I met a man at a restaurant in Burbank and he asked what I did so I gave him my business card. He ended up coming in for a reading that same evening. When I opened up the channel, I saw him clairvoyantly right away. He looked as he did in life but on his back were these stubby little nubs of wings that were gray and black. If you've ever seen the movie *Constantine* with Keanu Reeves, he looked like the Archangel Gabriel at the end. I told him what I saw and right away he confirmed that it was him, that he knew he was a fallen angel. It was a very intense reading actually. He was still in the early stages of trying to come back into the light and the dark did not want to release their hold on him, so I was getting psychically attacked throughout the entire reading.

The message for him was that he was to try to keep himself as pure as possible and focus on his mission. Only by doing this, could he gain his wings and his light back. It was going to take multiple lives; this was just the beginning of his journey. In particular, lust and an over focus on sex was one of his main struggles. This is one of the most seductive draws for fallen angels. Lust is what caused many of the angels to fall in the first place. It has taken me some time to understand the darkness of lust. Let me say first hand that love and lovemaking can be a wonderful thing, but lust that has no deep emotional connection and often is inspired by objectification, is quite dark energetically. When the physical and the spiritual connect through lovemaking, it can be magical. When the focus is purely on the physical, it's often hollow and can be quite damaging. Not all of the angels who mated with human women were fallen, some did so in a loving way, but that is a subject that would take a whole other book to cover. If you don't believe this happened then know that the biblical flood was supposedly created to kill the offspring of angel and man, the Nephilim. This man I read for was not Nephilim as he was in a human form, but his soul was angelic.

Even I am amazed sometimes when something comes up in a reading that seems so fantastical and the other person acknowledges it as if I said, "Today is Tuesday," or "good afternoon." But those who have unusual soul heritage often know they are different. If you've ever felt that you are not quite like everyone else, it is very likely true. As a child, I remember looking around and thinking, I don't see anyone like me. I want to be clear that one type of soul is not better than another, they are all simply different. A lion is not better than a flower and a kangaroo is not better than an alligator and a human is not better than an angel or vice versa. Each type of life and soul is wonderful and beautiful. Just as with humanity, diversity truly is so incredible and wonderful. It did, however give me a lot of peace of mind to understand why it was that I felt different. This idea might seem very wild, but I think that is mostly because we have been taught that the magical and the mystical are not real. The truth is the world is magic, all of it, and it all goes much more smoothly when we recognize the nature of the world. I encourage each and every one of you to connect with your own magic and the magic of the world. It truly is a beautiful, magical, complicated and amazing place.

Even though many of these stories I tell might be hard to believe, start with the possibility. Ask yourself, is this possible? Start to pay attention to the world for yourself. Question what you've been taught. As a people have gone through a sort of collective brainwashing, but we are in the process of opening our eyes, to truly waking up. It is a wonderful time to be alive! There will be many challenges coming up in the next several years for humanity, but there are many blessings that will result as well. It is time for us to be alive and awake and to truly see what is happening and also to understand the incredible possibilities. If during this tumultuous time, you feel shaken and scared, ask the angels to help and comfort you. The Archangels will always answer your prayers. As we all see the truth, release our fear, see through deception, and choose love, the entire world transforms.

Afterword

I want everyone to know that while not everyone may have the same gifts that I have, we all have ways of connecting and receiving information. Most of us are far more intuitive than we give ourselves credit for. I encourage everyone reading this book to start tuning in and learning more about what their own gifts are. The world will be a much easier place if we are all using and connecting with each other through the gifts that we were given. I wish each of you the best on your own journey and invite you to ask your spirit guides and angels to help you along the way.

I am sending love and light to you and hope you can move forward on your illuminated path with a better understanding of the spiritual realm.

With love,
Laura Powers

Helpful Terms

Angel – An angel is a spiritual being of light whose purpose is to guide and assist incarnated beings. The word means messenger and one of their main purposes is to take our messages to and from heaven.

Angel Communicator – Someone who can communicate through one or more senses (sight, hearing, feeling) with angels.

Automatic writing – A psychic ability in which the writer directly channels messages from spiritual beings through writing. In some cases, the writer may not even have knowledge of the words coming through them.

Channeling – To receive messages from spiritual beings and to relay the messages through speech or writing.

Claire senses – Psychic senses, clair is the French word for clear.

Clairalience – Clear smelling or receiving information from your sense of smell; also called clairsentience. This is a form of extra sensory perception or ESP.

Clairaudience – Clear hearing or hearing sounds that are not on the physical plane. This can be hearing a sound with your ears or hearing the word or phrase in your mind like a thought which isn't yours. This is a form of extra sensory perception or ESP.

Claircognizance – Clear knowing or knowing something you have no logical way of knowing. This is a form of extra sensory perception or ESP.

Clairgustance – The ability to taste something that you have not put in your mouth. This is a form of extra sensory perception or ESP.

Clairsentience – Clear feeling or feeling something coming from another source. This can be a physical sensation or emotion. This is a form of extra sensory perception or ESP.

Clairvoyance – Clear seeing or seeing something that is not on the physical plane. Clairvoyance can be experienced with your physical eyes or with your third or internal eye. This is a form of Extra Sensory Perception or ESP.

Cord – An energetic connection between people, places, and things which transmits energy and emotions.

Dark entity – A spiritual being whose intent and purpose is not of the light. Dark entities are like spiritual parasites and feed on and create negative energies such as pain, sorrow, depression, anxiety, or fear.

Demon – A supernatural energy being that feeds on and creates darkness in the world. This term is often used within the context of religion.

Devil – A dark and malevolent leader of hell and demons. Usually used within a Judeo-Christian context.

Empathy – The ability to feel what others are feeling. This is a form of Extra Sensory Perception or ESP.

Energy body – The energetic part of our body; we are made of matter and energy, and both parts come together to form us.

Entity – An energetic being that does not have a physical form. Entities are non-human and are not animals or angels either but some other type of being. There are many different types of entities.

EMF detector – An electromagnetic frequency detector. These devices can show evidence of paranormal activity.

EVPs (Electronic Voice Phenomenon) – Electronic recordings that are believed to capture sound caused by paranormal activity.

Extra Sensory Perception (ESP) – One or more heightened senses that perceive more than the normal range of sensing.

Ghost – An earth bound spirit or the spirit of a person whose body has died and whose soul or spirit has not crossed into the light.

Medium – Someone who can communicate with ghosts (earth bound spirits) and spirits (people without a body that are not earth bound).

Near-death experience (NDE) – A personal experience, in which a person experiences the continuation of their consciousness, even after the clinical death of their body.

Other side – The place where spirits reside once they cross into the light. Some people call it heaven.

Out-of-body experience (OBE) – A phenomenon in which an individual experiences their soul separating from their body. Usually the individual will then witness their body separately from them. The soul can then travel freely without the physical limitations of the body.

Paranormal – Events that are outside the realm of normal experience and cannot be explained by current science.

Parapsychology – A term coined in 1889 to describe research of the paranormal. Max Dessoir created the term by combining the words for "para" (which means alongside), with the word psychology. The clair-senses, precognition, telepathy, psychokinesis, ghosts, and other paranormal experiences are scientifically studied in parapsychology.

Precognition – Knowing something is going to happen before it does with no logical way of knowing so. This is a form of Extra Sensory Perception or ESP.

Psychic – Someone who received information from the non-physical realm.

Psychokinesis - The ability to move matter with your mind.

Psychometry – The ability to receive information from an object through touch.

Reiki – A type of energy healing in which healing energy is channeled through the practitioner into the individual being healed.

Reincarnation – The act through which our souls learn. Souls incarnate in a body and after they have died, review their life and plan the next one. For advanced souls, multiple incarnations may be possible simultaneously.

Remote viewing – A psychic exercise in which psychic looks at a place from a remote location.

Sage – A plant that can be used to clear negative or stagnant energy.

Shaman – A person who is trained to communicate and work with the spirit realm. Shamans are found in indigenous cultures throughout the world.

Shapeshifter – A supernatural being that can change form at will. A werewolf is a type of shapeshifter with only two forms. Some shapeshifters can take on any form they desire.

Spirit – The non-physical manifestation of a person or being. The spirit never dies and is made of energy.

Telepathy – The ability to communicate with others through thoughts.

Vampire – A supernatural life form that feeds on blood and energy.

Voodoo – A spiritual practice that combines the beliefs and traditions of the Haitian people, Native Americans, and the French and Spanish. Voodoo can be used to heal or curse people.

Sources

These are books and websites that I referenced for this book and that have informed me and my work:

Appleton, Nancy. *Suicide by Sugar*. Square One Publishers, 2008.

Backman, Linda. *Bringing Your Soul to Light*. Llewellyn Worldwide Ltd., 2009.

BPD Central. *Personality Disorders*. April, 2016. https://www.bpdcentral.com/faq/personality-disorders

BPD Central. Beauvoir: The Jefferson Davis Home and Presidential Library. March, 2016. *http://www.beauvoir.org/*

CNN. Colorado Shooting Fast Facts. December 5, 2015. http://edition.cnn.com/2013/07/19/us/colorado-theater-shooting-fast-facts/

Davis, William. The Wheat Belly Blog, November 2015. http://www.wheatbellyblog.com/

Davis, William. *Wheat Belly*. Rodale, 2014.

De Becker, Gavin. *The Gift of Fear*. Gavin De Becker, 2010.

Diamandis, Peter, and Kotler, Steven. *Abundance, the Future is Better Than You Think*. Free Press, 2012.

Denver Museum of Nature and Science. Ghenghis Khan Invades Denver. March, 2016. http://www.dmns.org/press-room/news-releases/genghis-khan-invades-denver/

Empowered Sustenance. *Why I quit Stevia*. November 2015. http://empoweredsustenance.com/is-stevia-bad-for-you/

Engaged Brains. *College Students and Alcoholism*. December, 2015. https://engaged-brains.wikispaces.com/Alcoholism+and+College+Students

Explorable. *Discovery of Bacteria*. March 2016. https://explorable.com/discovery-of-bacteria

Festival of Faerie. *Festival of Faerie: A Fae Folk Festival,* March, 2016. http://festivaloffaerie.com/

Grease the Musical. *Grease*. January 2015. http://www.greasethemusical.com/

Huffington Post. *Haunted Tour in New Orleans*. May 14, 2012. http://m.huffpost.com/us/entry/haunted-tour-in-new-orlea_b_1515062.html

Huffington Post. *The Deadly Neurotoxin Everyone Uses Daily*. August 4, 2010. http://www.huffingtonpost.com/dr-mercola/aspartame-health-risks_b_668692.html

IMDB. *Ghostbusters*. March 2016. http://www.imdb.com/title/tt0087332/

IMDB. *Lady Jane*. April 2016. http://www.imdb.com/title/tt0091374/

IMDB. *The Cable Guy*. March 2016.
http://www.imdb.com/title/tt0115798/

Loveline. *Loveline with Mike and Dr. Drew. December 2015.*
http://www.lovelineshow.com/

Mayo Clinic. *Narcissistic Personality Disorder.* December 2015.
http://www.mayoclinic.org/diseases-conditions/narcissistic-personality-disorder/basics/definition/con-20025568

McTaggart, Lynn. *The Intention Experiment: Using Your Thoughts to Change Your Life and the World.* Atria Books. 2007.

Medical Daily. *Long-Term Effects of Alcohol Impair Brain's Pathways That Underlie Impulse Control.* November, 2015.
http://www.medicaldaily.com/long-term-effects-alcohol-impair-brains-pathways-underlie-impulse-control-311242

Michaels, Jillian. *MYTH: Switching to Diet Soda Will Help Me Lose Weight.* March 2016.
http://www.jillianmichaels.com/fit/lose-weight/myth-diet-soda

NIH National Institute of Alcohol Abuse and Alcoholism. Alcohol's Damaging Effects on the Brain. December, 2016.
http://pubs.niaaa.nih.gov/publications/aa63/aa63.htm

Natural News. *The Hidden Dangers of Caffeine: How Coffee Causes Exhaustion, Fatigue, and Addiction.* March 2016.
http://www.naturalnews.com/012352_caffeine_coffee.html#

NBC News. *Oregon Shooting: Umpqua Gunman Chris Harper Mercer – What We Know.* December 2015.
http://www.nbcnews.com/storyline/oregon-college-

shooting/oregon-shooting-umpqua-gunman-chris-harper-mercer-what-we-know-n437351

Navarro, Joe. *What Every BODY is Saying*. Harper Collins Publishing, 2009.

Perlmutter, David. *Grain Brain: The Surprising Truth about Wheat, Carbs, and Sugar—Your Brain's Silent Killers*. Hachette Book Group, 2013.

Pinsky, Drew. *The Mirror Effect: How Celebrity Narcissism is Seducing America*. Harper Collins, 2009.

Psychology Today. *Is Celebrity Behavior Making You a Narcissist?* November 2015. https://www.psychologytoday.com/blog/millennial-media/201306/is-celebrity-behavior-making-you-narcissist

Rowling, J.K. *Harry Potter and the Philosopher's Stone*. Bloomsbury Children's, 2014.

Stanford Business. *Charles O'Reilly: Narcissists Get Paid More Than You Do*. April 2016. https://www.gsb.stanford.edu/insights/charles-oreilly-narcissists-get-paid-more-you-do

The Great Harry Houdini. *Houdini and the Supernatural. March 2016*. http://www.thegreatharryhoudini.com/occult.html

The New York Times. *Narcissist Celebrities*. March, 2015. http://www.nytimes.com/2006/12/10/magazine/10Section2b.t-5.html

The Telegraph. *San Bernadino Shooting: Isil Claims Attack as Reports Suggest Wife Came to US to Perpetrate Terror.*

December 2015
.http://www.telegraph.co.uk/news/worldnews/northamerica/usa/12030160/California-shooting-Multiple-victims-reported-in-San-Bernardino-live.html

Virtue, Doreen. *Earth Angels*. Hay House Publishing, 2002.

WebMD. *Celiac Disease*. December 2015.
http://www.webmd.com/digestive-disorders/celiac-disease/celiac-disease

Wikipedia. *2010 Chile earthquake.* December 2015.
https://en.wikipedia.org/wiki/2010_Chile_earthquake

Wikipedia. *Aneurysm*. March, 2016.
https://en.wikipedia.org/wiki/Aneurysm

Wikipedia. *Blind Men and Elephant Story*. March 2016.
https://en.wikipedia.org/wiki/Blind_men_and_an_elephant

Wikipedia. *Constantine*. December, 2015.
https://en.wikipedia.org/wiki/Constantine_(film)

Wikipedia. *Effects of Alcohol on Memory*. November, 2016.
https://en.wikipedia.org/wiki/Effects_of_alcohol_on_memory

Wikipedia. *Genghis Khan*. March, 2016.
https://en.wikipedia.org/wiki/Genghis_Khan

Wikipedia. *History of Virology*. November, 2015.
https://en.wikipedia.org/wiki/History_of_virology

Wikipedia. *Karen Horney*. November, 2016.
https://en.m.wikipedia.org/wiki/Karen_Horney

Wikipedia. *Lady Jane Grey.* November, 2015.
http://englishhistory.net/tudor/relative/lady-jane-grey/

Wikipedia. *Narcissus.* November, 2016.
https://en.wikipedia.org/wiki/Narcissus_(mythology)

Wikipedia. *Narcissism.* November, 2016.
https://en.wikipedia.org/wiki/Narcissism

Wikipedia. *Narcissistic Leadership.* April, 2016.
https://en.wikipedia.org/wiki/Narcissistic_leadership#Corporat
e_narcissism

Wikipedia. *November 2015 Paris Attacks.* November, 2015.
https://en.wikipedia.org/wiki/November_2015_Paris_attacks

Wikipedia. *Ouija.* March, 2016.
https://en.wikipedia.org/wiki/Ouija

Wikipedia. *Remote Viewing.* March, 2016.
https://en.wikipedia.org/wiki/Remote_viewing

Wikipedia. *San Bernadino Attack.* November, 2015.
https://en.wikipedia.org/wiki/2015_San_Bernardino_attack

Stay tuned for Laura's forthcoming book about *Archangels and Ascended Masters* and *The Supernatural Survival Guide*!

For additional information on Laura's psychic work, go to www.healingpowers.net. To receive updates about Laura's books, speaking engagements, events, TV show and more, submit your info on the subscribe page. For information on Laura's writing, modeling, acting, singing, hosting and other entertainment work, go to www.laurapowers.net.

About the Author – Laura Powers

Laura is a medium, angel communicator, ghost whisperer, actress, singer, model, and author of *Life and the After Life – Notes from a Medium and Angel Communicator, Angels: How to Understand, Recognize, and Receive their Guidance, Diary of a Ghost Whisperer,* and *Angels and Manifesting.* She received her bachelor's degree in theatre and her master's degree in political science from the University of Colorado. When she is not writing or traveling, you may find her singing, dancing, or exploring the unknown. You can find more information about her acting, singing and fiction writing on her website www.laurapowers.net. You can find more information about her work in this field on the website www.healingpowers.net. Laura is currently working on her next book and a screenplay.

77173118R00083

Made in the USA
Columbia, SC
29 September 2019